A
Love For
A Lifetime

"Waiting on God"

By

Shundra Yuille

Title: **A Love For A Lifetime**

Sub-Title: **Waiting on God**

Author: **Shundra Yuille**

Republished by S.I.T (Stand In Truth Publications)

info@comfortableinonesownskin.com

ISBN: 9798988853251

Printed in United States of America

Copyright © 2024 Shundra Yuille

Acknowledgements

First, I want to acknowledge the Lord Jesus Christ, who is my life source and the one who gave me the desire to put words to paper in the form of a story. Now, my story has become a book. I acknowledge my husband who said, "If this is what you desire to do, do it." I want to also recognize and give credit to my publisher, Melinda Walker. She brought this book to life.

Dedication

First and foremost, I dedicate this book to the Lord Jesus Christ, who has given me the passion to write. Next, I give honor to my loving husband and my amazing children who told me, "GO FOR IT!" Also, to my parents, Michael and Alice Lofton, and siblings who have always encouraged me to pursue my passion for creative writing. Finally, to my spiritual brother and sister, Pastor Kaderick and Lady Debra Michelle Jones, who read this book when it was in the initial stages on sheets of paper. They said, "Sister Yuille, why don't you open this book up and expound a little more?" Expounding is exactly what I did.

Table of Contents

Foreword

There are not many people in life God has allowed to come full circle in life with me, but Shundra has been one of the few that has. I knew from the time we met years ago; she was a God sent woman that was destined to greatness and for greatness. I can remember asking her to join my anthology and when I saw how efficient she was as a person; I knew I wanted her in my life. Shundra told me years ago that her dream was to become a number 1 best seller and she wanted her books to be on the shelves of the local library all the way up to Books A Million. I knew then she had a message that she wanted to share with the masses and that she had a passion to write.

Shundra gave me her manuscript a year before we started moving forward on her writing project. When I received the manuscript and started reading it, I was so very impressed. First, this was my very first Fiction book, I envisioned. I am so used to being one dimensional and only writing and coordinating Non-Fiction books. I was taken back by this Fiction book. Secondly it was a love story and Thirdly it was a Novel. I said to myself, this girl has a lot to offer the world.

Shundra has a vivid imagination that puts you at the scene of each chapter. Shundra is multifaced and is not a one-dimensional type of person and that brought pure joy to me.

I said to Shundra what made you publish a Fiction as your first book? Why did you choose the characters you chose? How did you come up with the title, "A Love For A Lifetime"? I asked, is this based on a true story? Well, all these questions will be answered when I interview Shundra. This is just the tip of the iceberg for her, and she is already working on part 2 of this amazing novel.

This novel is not only for married couples to give hope to them but also for those who desire to be married one day. Reading this book will provoke your mind and heart. This book will provoke your thought process and decision making. I was just thinking today, over 30 years ago I had not imagined I would have love for a lifetime. Did I even put any thought into the decision I made to marry at 19 years of age? Did I have a goal for my marriage? Did I know the difference between love and lust? These are the thought provoking questions "A Love For A Lifetime" will ask each of us as the readers.

As I close my message about the author, I must inject, Shundra is not an ordinary lady. Shundra is an extra ordinary lady that has an extra ordinary message about love. Shundra wants the world to know that Love can last for a lifetime when we make the right choices by asking the right questions.

Melinda Walker

Finally There, LLC

DBA Stand In Truth Publications (S.I.T)

Introduction

Janette Oake, Karen Kingsbury, Ted Dekkar, Watchman Nee, E. M. Bounds, and Max Lucado (just to name a few) are some of my favorite authors who inspire me to write. All my favorite authors' books speak the truth and tell a story. Because I am a visual reader, when I read, I see myself walking through the pages of the story with the author.

The idea of writing the book you are currently reading came to me in 2010. Initially, I wrote the story in a tiny book that had blank pages inside of it. I received it from a vendor at a teacher's convention. Yes, I still have that book today. Honestly, I talked about wanting to become an author and sharing my story in a book at the close of an open house meeting for a school my children attended.

One of my dear friends, who has become a brother to me, is a pastor and was present at the meeting. My friend asked me if he could read what I had written. At first, I was very hesitant. I double-checked just to ensure he was serious. As I proceeded to hand over the book, everything within me began to shake and tremble nervously.

About a month or so later, he gave me the book back with some feedback. The feedback he gave me became the driving force

I needed to finish my book. His words to me were, "Sister Yuille, why did you shorten it? Open it up and elaborate more."

I was floored that someone of his stature took an interest in something I wrote. Every now and then when he passed me at school, he would check on my progress. Finally, in April of 2013, yes, three years later, the quest towards writing my book began.

Just to let you in on what sparked my interest in becoming an author. It was listening to people read to me at a young age and learning to read and write myself. During my teenage years, I wrote a lot of poems. Also, during my junior year in high school, I took a computer literacy class taught by Mrs. Emma Rawls. Most days she told us to write a short story. She would walk around to everyone's computer to see what we were writing and how close we were to completion. I remember a few times she asked me if I had ever sent or thought about sending my short stories to Guidepost. I told her no. At that time, I did not think my short stories were Guidepost worthy. Apparently, Mrs. Rawls did. Ever since that day, I have wanted to write a book.

Fast forward a few years. I married and began having children. We would take the children to the downtown library to check out books. I enjoyed reading, and I wanted my children to enjoy reading as well. This is how I met some of my favorite authors. While reading some of the books we checked out at the library, I often thought to myself what it would be like to write my own book. I thought about writing a children's book with colorful fun pages. What would I write on those pages? I thought about writing a book on angels. Immediately, I thought to myself that was not it.

As I reread the book I wrote several times, romance came to mind. I said within myself, "There is a lot of love in this book. *A Love for A Lifetime*. Yes, that is it.

Since marriage, I have always wanted my children's names in whatever book I write. I saw this book as relaxing writing. I did not have to struggle to make up many of the characters' names because some of them were my children's names. While making some revisions to the manuscript, I noticed some of the personalities of the characters strongly resembled my own children. Honestly, this was not intentional. Furthermore, I chose to write a fiction book to step out of the box somewhat, to take a leap of faith, and venture out to do something I have never done before. Writing this book was truly exciting and exhilarating. So, take a seat. Sit back, relax, and sip on your coffee, tea, wine, or whatever you drink. Allow this book to take you to another place.

CHAPTER 1:
Who Is She?

This story began in Manchester, Arkansas. Traffic was totally backed up, and there was no way around it. It was a beautiful summer morning, and the water was glistening in the river.

Mason exclaimed, "This would have been a nice morning to take a walk on the bridge!" But he was on his way to work. Mason had no idea what important event was going to happen today. Let me share a snippet about who Mason is. He was deemed the perfect gentleman. He was currently a single man; however, around five years ago he was engaged to be married to his ex-fiancée, Eboni Cutler. What would have been a union was short-lived because she believed the Lord was keeping them for someone else. She was adamant that he was destined to be with another woman and vice versa. They were not the match made in heaven!

During their time together, Mason and Eboni went house hunting, and they picked out the most beautiful family home. Even though they did not get married, and they both moved on, so to speak, he still liked the house.

After the engagement was over, he took most of his savings and put a down payment into it. This was where he now lived. It was a nice four-bedroom, three-bathroom, two-car garage home with the amenities any woman would enjoy. Some features included hardwood floors throughout the house, except the bathrooms. They had tile floors. The house was also equipped with a massive master bedroom with an ensuite, hot tub, covered swimming pool, nice flower beds, big back, side, and front yards, and a nice, long driveway.

Fast forward to the morning of work, he woke up at five o'clock and immediately was out of bed and on his knees. He prayed, "Lord, I thank You for waking me this morning and for giving me a mind to come to You before I do anything else. I thank You for being Lord of Lords and King of Kings. I appreciate You for protecting me and those around me. I pray You bless those in authority around the world and in other nations. I thank You that You see it fit for me to be in the position that I am in at my job, and I pray Your continued blessings on the ones further down the chain of command. Lord, help me to set a Christ-like example for my coworkers." Mason continued in intercession until approximately six-thirty that morning. What Mason was not in the know about was that, on this specific day, the Lord was going to start answering his prayers concerning some things he had prayed about some days ago concerning himself.

As Mason got dressed for work, he was still anxious about how his day was going to be even though he prayed. That stirred him to be in constant prayer, saying, "Lord, help me today. Help me to not be an offense to others today at work. I just got this new position, so help me, Lord."

Mason was promoted the day before to an executive position at his job. He was now a Certified Public Accountant (CPA) for one of the largest corporations in Arkansas, Murphy's Investment Incorporated. Every day he would go to work, before now, it would be him just doing what he does and what he knows he can do. Not fully depending on God. Recently, he began to really pray and ask God to take him to another level. He prayed again, "Lord, help me to walk in righteousness and true holiness and not just let every day be the same thing over and over again. I really desire now for there to be a change in the atmosphere at my job and for the corporation to glorify the work of Your kingdom."

Well, off Mason went to work. On his way, he decided to drive the cheaper route, which was across town over a bridge. Mason arrived at work and noticed someone had parked in his favorite parking spot. He immediately spotted another parking spot a little closer to the door of the office building, and so he parked in that spot, not noticing the car parked beside him. As he got out of his car, he grabbed his briefcase from the backseat and walked into the building.

While walking through the corridor Mason greeted everyone as usual. "Good morning, Jessie."

"Morning, Mason," Jessie replied.

"Good morning, Jody."

"What's up, Mason?" Jody asked.

"Just getting ready for what I know is going to be a great day," Mason responded. "What's up Joseph?" Mason asked.

"Just living the life, Mason, living the life," Joseph answered.

Moving over to the other side of the corridor is Miranda. "Good morning, Miranda," said Mason.

"Good morning, Mason," Miranda said.

"Morning, Nicholas," Mason said.

"Morning, Mason," said Nicholas.

Making his way into his office, Mason's eyes glanced down the corridors. He was glued to the neatly shaped body of a woman who had shoulder-length, curly hair. This beauty was dressed in a black and gold pant suit with an exquisite pair of gold heels. Mason was not the type to stare, so he quickly went into his office and started to prepare himself for the day's workload. He started his day with working on some investments for his clients.

As he got settled, there was a knock on his office door. "Mrs.

Ingleton is early," he thought to himself. She was a client he was expecting later that day.

He walked over, opened the door, and, to his surprise, there stood Mr. Murphy and the young woman he had glanced at in the corridor earlier. Mr. Charles Murphy was the owner of this company, Murphy Investments Incorporated. He started this company seven years ago. When he heard about Mason through a mutual friend, he had to have him in his company. "Good morning, Mason," Mr. Murphy said.

"Good morning, Mr. Murphy. Come on in." Mason beckoned to both his guests. He closed the door behind them after they came in. Typical of Mason when he had a client, he went over to the table where he and his clients would normally sit in order to do their investment plans. He pulled out a chair for the young lady and then went to the other side of the table to take his seat. He and Mr. Murphy then sat down.

"Mason, this is Danielle Belkin. She has come to us from another investment company. Danielle has been working for another company, but their senior executive was accused of and found guilty of fraud and embezzlement. After hearing about our company, she immediately applied and was hired for the job. Moving forward, I am pairing her with you because she was doing the same work at that investment company that you do here for us. I hope that this will not cause a problem?" Mr. Murphy stated.

Mason then responded, "Oh no, Mr. Murphy, this will not be a problem at all. This is actually an amazing idea because now I will have someone to share the workload with."

Mr. Murphy smiled and said, "Her office will be across the hallway from you. If you do not have a client coming in anytime soon, you can show her some of your caseloads now."

With a wide smile, Mason answered, "This is perfect timing because I won't have a client coming in for the next couple of hours."

"Well, Mason and Danielle, I have a meeting to attend upstairs. I will be available if any help is needed; however, I trust you both will be fine because both of you are superb at what you do. If for any reason you need my help with something, don't hesitate to give me a call."

Mason then stood up to open the door, but Mr. Murphy said, "Mason, you can sit back down. I will let myself out." And that's exactly what he did.

When his boss was through the door, Mason walked over to his desk and grabbed a stack of papers that were already paperclipped together. He then went back to the table, sat back in his chair, and began to explain to Danielle the investment plan he had which belonged to Mr. Jacob Hughes, one of his clients. Every now and then he would look up and look at her face and ask, "Do you understand why I did his plan this way?" Danielle would respond and give him feedback.

For the first hour they were able to go through and make some changes on the investment plans for three clients.

"Mason, I hate to disturb our work time, but where is the restroom?" Danielle asked.

"Oh, it is outside my office door, two doors down the hallway to your right." He stood up and said, "Let me get that for you." He came rushing around the table, like the perfect gentleman he was, to help with her chair.

When she stood up, they looked into each other's eyes as Danielle's mouth sounded the words, "I will be right back."

"I will grab us another stack of clients' investment plans until you get back," Mason stuttered.

She walked out the door and closed it behind her.

He then grabbed the stack of papers from his desk and sat back in his chair while looking up to the ceiling. "Lord, I know that You probably find this humorous. She is beautiful on the outside, and she seems to be beautiful on the inside too, but You know I will have to check that out. Lord, You are good. I trust You with all things," exclaimed Mason.

It wasn't long after that, Danielle walked back into the office and said, "Alright, back to these investment plans." She sat down, and they got back to business as usual.

Two hours later, they were going back and forth across the hall to one another's office to discuss the different investment budgets and plans. Mrs. Ingleton, who was slated to be Mason's first client, called and rescheduled, so Mason's next appointment was not until two that afternoon. He immediately made plans for lunch with his new buddy. "Danielle, I am a bit hungry, what about you? I am going to order take out from Gangum Chinese, would you like anything?" Mason asked.

"Do you have a menu on hand from them?" she asked.

"Yes, I do!" he quickly declared. He got the menu off his desk and went across the hallway to her office to share it.

"Wow, they have so many choices. This Bok Choy soup with fried noodles is going to give me life," she said with a chuckle.

"Is that what you want?"

"Yes," she answered.

"What about something to drink?" he asked.

"Yes, and how is their lemonade?"

"I like their lemonade because it is not overly sweet, and they use freshly squeezed lemons," he shared.

"Well, I will try that for sure."

Mason then asked, "Do you want a dessert with your meal?" to which Danielle responded no. She was sure the soup and noodles would be enough for her. He called and placed the order and was informed it would be delivered in about thirty minutes. They continued to work on their caseload until their lunch arrived.

Mason walked into his office, closed the door, sat down, and placed his hands behind his head. "Who is she?" he thought as he reclined in his office chair.

CHAPTER 2:
Hard Work Pays Off

Meanwhile, across town, Eboni Cutler had opened the doors to her hair and nails salon, and she was busy with her partners and clients. Mason and Eboni were engaged to be married five years ago, but about two weeks before their wedding, they believed God spoke to them about being married to other persons. This meant Mason was to marry someone else, and Eboni was to marry someone else. However, for the past year Eboni had been saying that she no longer believed it was God while Mason was adamant that he knew it was God.

On a busy workday, Eboni was greeted by her three best friends. "Hey, E, looks like you guys are busy today," said Hope.

"Hey, what's going on, Hope, Shannon, and Cherish? I missed you guys this weekend," explained Eboni. Shannon also worked in the salon with Eboni.

"We missed you too, and we said we are going to the next hair show no matter where it is."

"When is it, and how did the last hair show go this past weekend?" Hope asked.

"I enjoyed it to the max! I hoped Mason could have been there to see me in action. There were a lot of product vendors and a lot of hairstylists and hair colorists. It was fabulous," Eboni responded.

Cherish was curious and decided to ask Eboni, "When are you going to let Mason go, and what if he already has another friend? A woman friend he is interested in, to be specific."

Rolling her eyes, Eboni explained, "The only friend he has that is a woman is me."

Hope immediately told Cherish to let Eboni be and don't start no mess.

"Anyway, what do you ladies want to do about lunch?" Eboni asked.

"Let's go to El Porton, the Mexican restaurant," said Shannon.

Eboni then turned to one of her salon partners and mentioned that she would be back in a couple hours and off the ladies went.

At El Porton, Eboni and the ladies sat down to have their lunch. They marveled at how great the food tasted. Shannon even stated she was pleased with the settings and the fact that everything was buffet style. At the restaurant, the decorations looked and made you feel like you were in Mexico or on some Mexican island. "I feel like I am on the coast of Mexico. Where is the sand?"

chuckled Eboni.

They finished up their lunches and went back to the salon. Eboni only had an hour and a half before her next client.

When she got back to the salon, she sat in a chair and said, "Oh, my goodness. I believe I ate too much. I am ready to take a nap."

"Well, you do have an hour and a half before your next client. Just go to the back and take a forty-five-minute power nap," Shannon suggested. Eboni took her friend up on the idea and went to the back to take a power nap.

After her nap, Eboni's client, Mrs. Lane, arrived for a shampoo. In deep thought, Eboni thought to herself, "Wow, hard work sure does pay off because Mrs. Lane has been coming to my salon since it opened two years ago."

Mrs. Lane also told her friends about Eboni's salon, and once a month, she brought a few of her friends for a girl date, to get their hair and nails done. In the middle of washing Mrs. Lane's hair, she began planning with Mrs. Lane. She assured her she was all set for her next hair appointment.

"I am looking at the middle of the month. I will get with my ladies to see what date will be better for them and let you know. I know I need to let you know in advance because of the number of ladies," Mrs. Lane stated.

In confirmation, Eboni nodded and said, "Yes, please do because I close the salon for that day so that you and the ladies can have a real girl date. I also need to know so that I can make sure that those who I want to work with you and the ladies will be available to work on that day."

Mrs. Lane's friends really enjoyed the treatment they received when they came to Eboni's salon. So much so, that one of the ladies asked her if they could do a girl date twice a month.

Back at the investment firm, Mason and Danielle had received their lunch and were grubbing. "Mason, thank you for lunch. The food was great, and this lemonade is amazing. I am going to have to get a menu so that I can order again when I'm at home too," said Danielle.

Mason being a big fan of the lemonade, began to explain to Danielle that he often uses it to power himself up so that he can get through his workdays without feeling hungry.

"Do you work out a lot?" Danielle asked Mason, who immediately responded, "Yeah, only three to four times a week." Danielle shared she believed she was getting to where she wants to be as far as her health is concerned, as she too frequents the gym weekly. She often goes two to three times a week. As the two shared their views on a healthy lifestyle, they both realized they had somewhat of a similar technique. They believed in eating as healthily as possible during the week and having a cheat day on the weekend.

After some time in dialogue, they both went back to completing their assigned task. Mason specifically because he had three different clients who were coming to his office to discuss their investment plans. It was customary for Mason to have Danielle in his office to listen to the conversations between himself and his client because she was still being trained. On many occasions too, he would allow her to attend to and assist him with his clients.

After ending his meeting, in came Mr. Murphy from upstairs, flaunting a huge smile. He walked into Mason's office as both him and Danielle were wrapping up their conversation with a client. They were adjusting a client's investment plan and talking about how they could revise some parts of it. As they acknowledged their boss, they stood up to welcome him in. Mr. Murphy then beckoned to Mason that he wanted to speak with him alone for a moment.

Danielle immediately grabbed some of the plans and documents from Mason's desk and headed to her office.

"Danielle, I will only be a moment, so you know what, you can stay because what I have to say pertains to both of you," uttered Mr. Murphy.

Danielle made a U-turn and sat back down at the desk.

"Well, as you two know, I just finished a meeting with some men who appreciate how we have helped them and others. Now they are constantly referring our business to many who need our expertise. Danielle, even though this is your first day, you get in on a raise."

In shock, Mason looked at Mr. Murphy. "A raise? Wow!"

Danielle was also surprised as Mr. Murphy looked at her and said, "Yes, young lady, here hard work truly pays off."

Mason looked at her and held his hand out to give her a congratulatory handshake. When she puts her hand in his, reluctantly, he shook her hand and said, "Welcome to Murphy's Investments!" to which she replied, "Thank you."

Mr. Murphy then spoke to them about his meeting and the conditions of the raise.

Mason sighed and in a low voice uttered, "Wow, today has been amazing." They both thanked each other for being able to work together efficiently to make the workload.

Danielle also shared, "Mason, you are a beast at this

investment planning. You go into beast mode when it comes to this paperwork. I am thankful that I get a chance to work with you and learn new ways to budget a client's funds and better ways to help a client invest his or her funds."

He thanked her for the compliment. "What time do you come in tomorrow, Danielle?" Mason asked.

She replied, "I come in at nine o'clock in the morning."

"Alright." He responded. Immediately, he grabbed his briefcase and left out his office door.

He met Danielle at the elevator. While on the elevator, they discussed the names of the clients that they needed to see in the morning. After getting off the elevator, they went to the time clock. Mason showed her how to clock out, and they prepared to walk to their cars and head home. When they walked out the door of the building, Mason said, "Alright, I will see you tomorrow."

She looked at him and said "Yes, tomorrow."

As they walked to their cars, they looked at each other and chuckled after noticing that they were parked beside each other.

Mason explained, "Wow, I did not even notice a different car beside my car this morning."

"Yes, this is my Yota girl. She is my Toyota Corolla."

They smiled at each other as they got into their cars. Being the perfect gentleman, Mason waited until she left her parking space then he rolled out.

CHAPTER 3:
How Do I Handle Her?

On the way home, Mason's cell phone rang. It was Temperance, his oldest and only biological sister. They warmly exchanged greetings, then his sister said, "Good evening, Bro. How are you?"

"Hey, Sis. Everything is great!" answered Mason.

"I was just calling to let you know that we are coming to visit you this weekend," said Temperance.

He had no biological brothers, so he was beyond excited to hear from his sissy. "That is great! I am ready to see my nieces and my brother." Mason exclaimed. He referred to Temperance's husband as his brother because he was not fond of the term "brother-in-law." He said there was no closeness in the phrase "in-law." Mason tended to spoil the kids, so Temperance made sure to warn him about spoiling them, but Mason could not make any promises. "I will have special things planned for them all day Saturday," he said.

"Mason, I don't know why I even mentioned anything about them getting spoiled because you never listen to what I say," she said while laughing.

"Alright, Sis. Give my nieces a kiss for me. Give my brother a fist bump for me also, and I will talk with you later this week," Mason said before hanging up.

A few moments later, Mason arrived home. He parked his car outside the garage. He checked his mailbox and unlocked the door to his house. Once inside, he went straight to his bedroom to change clothes so he could leave for the gym. Mondays, Wednesday, and Fridays were his workout days, and (seldom) he might work out on a Saturday.

After he got dressed, he called his friends Quintin and Jason. They all exercised together on those days. Sure enough, both Jason and Quintin were ready, so Mason told them he would meet them at the gym.

Mason's house was closer to the gym, so when he arrived, he sat in his car and waited for his friends. Five minutes later, Quintin showed up and about two minutes after that Jason pulled in. Once out of their cars, Mason asked, "What's up guys? Are y'all ready for this workout? You know we have some competitions coming up in a couple of months." All three men competed in different five-mile races in different cities and states, so the gym time was preparation for the upcoming races.

"Yes, and we will be ready," Quintin and Jason said.

"Well, let's get it." Mason said, as they walked into the gym.

Mason, Jason, and Quintin were in beast mode as they worked out. They also had a personal trainer whose name was Greg. Greg was not in the gym today, but he gave them a list of things to do during their workout session. During the sessions, they always pushed to go beyond the goals that Greg had listed for them. They had their mind set on winning the next two races and to be a part of the marathon in New York.

"Yes! "We did it again," Jason said after completing and shattering their sets.

"Only up from here, guys, and I know that we can be in New York this year," said Mason.

Quintin added, "We can, and we will."

"YES!" they said in unison.

They then went to the locker room to shower before they went home.

After they showered, they discussed for a minute about the next time they would get together to work out and about their time to run five miles together. They finished up their conversation in their vehicles before driving off.

On the way home, Mason was listening to worship music by Hillsong. As he was singing along and worshipping, he was reminded of the raise he received today. Tears began to slowly slide down his cheeks, and he began to thank God for being a faithful God. Mason is a tither and a giver, so he was sure to always be on the receiving end, as God poured out favor on him.

When he arrived home, he parked his car inside the garage and just sat there for a moment worshipping God. He then said to God, "I thank You that You are awesome and faithful. Thank You for all that You continue to do for me. You are amazing and awesome. You are my life and my life changer. I glorify and praise You." He continued to thank God.

After a few minutes, Mason got out of his car and went inside the house. By this time, it was seven o'clock, so Mason grabbed a quick bite before going to bed. He remembered that he went by the store yesterday and bought a salad mix, so he fixed a salad and drank some water with it. He looked through his mail that came in today, and he looked at some paperwork that he brought home from work.

Meanwhile, back at the salon Eboni was talking with Shannon. "Shannon, I am one tired sister."

After inquiring, Shannon found out Eboni had two more clients for the day: Mrs. Landry at five and Miss Moss at six.

"Well, I am on my last client now, and I have to get out of here because my nephews have games this evening at seven. They play baseball for a youth league," Shannon explained.

Eboni was also a sports fan, so she said to Shannon, "Bring me a schedule, and maybe one day I can show up at one of their games. I started playing t-ball when I was four and went on to softball when I was in high school. I would love to come to a few of their games."

Shannon responded, "I will get a schedule from their mom this evening. I believe they will love hearing you cheer them on."

Shannon finished with her client and got her things together to leave. Shannon, being concerned, asked Eboni if she would be in the shop alone after she left, to which she replied, "No, Amora will be back because she has two more clients also, and you know if no one else was going to be here I would be leaving with you right now."

As soon as Shannon left, Eboni locked the door behind her. She always took precautions when she was in the salon by herself. Not long after, her last client, Miss Moss, arrived for her appointment. Eboni shampooed and placed her under the dryer.

As she sat waiting for Miss Moss hair to be dried, she started to have flashbacks about Mason and wondered what he might be up to. She often thought about calling him since he did not have her new number. At this point, it was seven-thirty, and she knew for sure he was not asleep yet. She decided to call him to see what he had been doing. Eboni had always kept Mason's number written in her address book, so she hoped he still had the same number.

She grabbed her cell phone and gave him a call. "Well, I see you still have the same number. How are you Mason, my love?" Eboni said after Mason answered.

"Is this Eboni Cutler?" he said.

"Yes, it is, my darling Mason," Eboni answered.

Mason was confused at the way Eboni was speaking, and he did not hesitate to ask her why she was talking in that manner.

She answered, "Because I love you, and I know you love me."

Then he said, "Yes, I do love you as a friend. How have you been doing?"

Eboni explained she was doing great and that she was just at the salon wondering if they could get together to catch up with one another and reminisce about the good ole days.

Mason, on the other hand, was not interested and rejected her idea of them reuniting. He was glad she called but didn't believe it would be a good idea for them to hook up for any reason. "Eboni, you know we can only be friends, and that is it. We have already tried the more-than-friends way, and God said no to that. We just have to be okay with just being friends," he firmly stated.

Eboni was extremely devastated because she felt otherwise. She was adamant that Mason was only saying that because he really did not want to be with her.

Mason quickly saved her new number and decided to end the conversation by saying, "Eboni, I am going to have to go. Again, I thank you for calling me, and I will have to talk with you on another day."

"Okay, Mason, I will let you think about what I said, and I will talk to you at another time. Bye, my love," said Eboni. They ended the call.

Mason was so disturbed, he had to go into prayer. "Lord, how do I handle this? I do not have feelings for Eboni like that anymore. I need Your help with this. Why is she calling me after two years of me not even knowing if she is even alive? God, I know there is a purpose for all things, but what is the purpose for this?"

Mason washed out the bowl and fork he used for his salad, dried them, and put them away. He made sure that all the lights that should be off in the front of his house were off and then he went to his room to get ready for bed. While in bed, Mason was still disturbed about Eboni's call and just laid there and prayed about it again.

As the night went on, he tossed in the bed, in and out of sleep. At one point, he woke up sweating profusely. He began to pray again. "Lord, I need Your help. I cannot shake this. Why has this disturbed me so much? Do I still have feelings for her that I am trying to suppress? If so, Lord take those feelings from me because I desire to do Your will. Satan, I rebuke you in Christ Jesus' name. Flee now." Then he fell asleep.

Eboni knew she had gotten under Mason's skin and believed she had him right where she wanted him and, at some point, he was going to give in and want to be more than just friends again. She finished up Miss Moss's hair after which she and Amora ensured the salon was swept and clean before they left out the door. It was time to say goodnight for the day. Both she and Amora went their separate ways after getting to their cars.

Eboni arrived home around nine that night. She parked her vehicle in the garage and went inside her house. This home was not as big as the one she would have shared with Mason, but it was big enough for more than her and four to five others to live in. Her house had a huge living room and kitchen area. It also carried three bedrooms and three bathrooms. The biggest bedroom was the master bedroom, which was her bedroom. It had a full bath and a nice sized walk-in closet.

Exhausted from a long day, she sat her purse on the kitchen counter and went through her mail while eating the salad she got earlier that day. She finished her salad and went to take a shower.

After her shower, she got on her knees and prayed, "Lord, help Mason to see that he needs me, and I need him. I know what we believed some years ago, but God, I believe it is time for us to reunite. I pray this in Your son Christ Jesus' name amen." While getting off her knees and into her bed, she thought to herself, "I hope you are thinking about me, Mason, my love."

Immediately, she fell asleep.

CHAPTER 4:
Prayer Makes The Difference

The next morning, Mason woke up feeling refreshed and rested. He got on his knees and prayed, "Lord, I thank You for making me free and for taking away the disturbance I had. I pray that You will move by Your Spirit today at my job and that You will perform through me. Strengthen me so that I can be someone else's strength. Lord, give Danielle and me wisdom in how to help our clients in every way today. You have always been my help, but today I'm desiring extra help. I need more of You today, Lord. God, I am thankful for Mr. Murphy, and I pray Your continued blessings upon him. I thank You now for answering my prayers in Your son Jesus Christ's name. Amen."

Following that, Mason got himself an amazing shower before going down to the kitchen. For breakfast, he started a pot of coffee and placed five eggs in a boiler to boil. He then hurried to his room to get dressed for work. Once he was dressed, he went and had his coffee and eggs that were brewed and boiled.

With his coffee in a mug and his eggs seasoned in a container, he grabbed his briefcase and was out the door to his car.

On the other side of town, Eboni was also up early. She too prayed and showered and then ventured to the kitchen to have her first meal of the day. Her breakfast consisted of coffee, a small pot of cheese grits, two scrambled eggs, and a few strips of bacon. She was happy that the Lord woke her up early enough to cook some breakfast for herself.

Glancing at the clock, she kept track of the time. It was only seven-thirty, and her first client would be at the salon at ten o'clock that morning.

Since it was still early, Eboni decided to eat and do her devotional. She got her book, sat at the table, fixed her plate, and a cup of orange juice alongside the coffee, and delved into her devotional.

Following her devotional reading, Eboni got dressed and fixed her hair and makeup. She whispered to herself, "I have to look good just in case I run into Mason." Quickly grabbing her purse, she left out the door heading across town to her salon.

Eboni made it to the salon one hour earlier than she had planned.

At the salon, Shannon was shampooing a client's hair, and three others who worked there also had their clients in the chair.

Eboni smiled and said, "So we are booming today!"

Shannon said, "E, you know that's what we do."

Chuckling, she confirmed that was exactly how things should be. Eboni started getting shampoos and conditioners and her work tools ready for when her clients came in. She knew that she had a full day, but she would be able to take a lunch break. Once she was ready, in walked her first client of the day.

Ten blocks away from Mason's home, Danielle was up and thanking God for a peaceful night and for her new job. She, like everyone else's morning routine, went to the kitchen to get her coffee started before she showered.

After her shower, she fixed herself some breakfast. On her breakfast menu was a small pot of rice, a few strips of bacon, and half of an orange.

Back at the kitchen table she ate breakfast and enjoyed her morning devotional reading. She always kept her devotional book on a rack beside her table. Danielle finished her breakfast and devotional, got dressed, and was out the door to work with her purse and briefcase in hand.

At Murphy's Investment Corporation, Mason and Danielle had been able to go over two of Danielle's clients' investment plans and had made the necessary adjustments.

Thirty minutes after they looked over both clients' paperwork,

Mason's client Mrs. Hope Albis, showed up for her ten o'clock appointment. Mrs. Albis has been coming to Mason for her investment planning and budgeting since the third day he started to work for the company. She had also spoken the word of God to him and over him. He was always happy to see her once or twice a month.

When Mrs. Albis came into Mason's office, Danielle was there with him. He asked Mrs. Albis if it was okay for Danielle to sit in to help them work through her investment plan. She told him sure, and she seemed excited about it. "You know, young lady, Mr. Mason here is a good man, and he needs a good woman. Are you a good woman?" Mrs. Albis asked.

"Mrs. Albis, why are you getting things started? Can we please handle your investment business? Danielle and I have not become good friends yet, and you already have us as more than friends," he said with an awkward smile.

Mason had truly become like a son to Mrs. Albis, who just wanted to see him happy with a wife and maybe a few children one day. Mason looked at Mrs. Albis and said, "I will put what you are saying to prayer because you know, prayer makes the difference."

Danielle had an unusual look on her face, so Mrs. Albis apologized for making her uncomfortable. With all that out of the way, they started addressing the investment plan and adjusted as needed.

Mason had two other clients after Mrs. Albis. By then he was famished. "I am going to Chick-fil-A for lunch. Do you want anything, Danielle?" he asked.

"No, thank you. I am going downstairs to the café. I do thank you for the offer though," she said.

They both got on the elevator and talked about the clients that they will have after lunch and the little time they will have to strategize about their plans.

When the elevator stopped on the first floor, they got off, and Mason walked Danielle to the café before heading to his lunch spot.

Back at the salon, Eboni finished the hair of the client she was working on. She told Shannon she was going to lunch. "Shannon, I am going to lunch. Do you want me to get you anything?"

"It all depends on where you are going, Eboni."

"I am going to the Chick-fil-A downtown," she replied.

"Well, no. I just don't have a taste for that today. I will just go after I'm finished with my client," Shannon explained.

Eboni went to the restroom of the salon where she freshened up, grabbed her purse, and left for her one-hour break.

CHAPTER 5:
Lord, I Need You To Do It

Pulling up to the downtown Chick-fil-A, Eboni was beyond happy. The drive-thru line was extremely long, so she decided to dine in for lunch. She walked in and approached the counter. There were three people in front of her, and the person to the right side of the counter was now receiving their order.

Now at the counter and being served, Eboni ordered a cobb salad with a large Arnold Palmer; that is a tea and lemonade mix. While she waited for her food, she noticed a face that she dared to believe she saw in her peripheral vision. She said to herself, "That cannot be Mason Taylor, not on this side of town!"

As she got closer to the table where he was, she noticed that it was really him. "Mason Taylor, is that really you?" she said. He looked up, noticed it was Eboni, then asked her how she was doing. "I am fine. May I dine with you at this table, Mason?"

Reluctantly, Mason said sure as he pulled the chair out for her to sit.

Eboni was overly excited to see Mason. After all, they had not seen each other in person in a couple of years.

During lunch, he questioned her about how she was doing and

the salon.

"I have been doing fabulous, and yes, I still have the salon, and it is doing fabulous also. How have you been doing, my love?" Eboni replied.

"I am doing well, and you do not have to say the 'my love' thing. I have also been promoted to an executive position at an investment firm. I am abundantly blessed," Mason shared.

Despite the kind words being exchanged, Eboni only had one thing on her mind. She believed they were supposed to be together at this time. She also thought that the Lord was saying for them to wait years ago but now was the right time. She still cared about him, but he had his mind focused somewhere else.

He firmly explained, "Eboni, as I have told you before, we can only be friends and nothing more. Yes, I still love you and care for you, but that's only on a friendship level. I believe what the Lord told us back then, and so it still stands right now."

"Mason, why are you talking like this? What is going on with you?" she asked.

Mason was clearly ready to end the conversation and leave. "Can we finish our lunch and go?" he said. They finished their lunch in silence. After they finished, he took their trash, told her thank you for sitting with him for lunch, and went to the door.

Still being persistent, she said, "Mason, can you see me tomorrow night at the Olive Garden for a date?"

"Eboni, only friends, nothing more. I will see you."

As he stood holding the door, she rubbed her body against his and told him she knew they were meant to be.

"Eboni, I will see you at another time. Have a nice afternoon," he said as he walked off to his car.

In the back, Eboni was still trying to get his attention, but he shook his head in disdain and got in his car.

Eboni got in her car and went back to work at the salon. On her drive, she thought "Mason knows he wants me, and he still has feelings for me as a girlfriend or fiancée. I don't know why he is acting this way towards me?"

While in deep thought, her cell phone rang. It was her client whose appointment was in about twenty minutes. She was calling to let her know that she would be about fifteen minutes later than expected. Eboni made it back to the salon. She put her purse in the back, and she came to the front and sat on the couch with Shannon. She was so eager to share what happened at lunch. "Shannon, guess who I had lunch with? Mason, my love! And he was such a gentleman. He said we can only be friends, but I know he wants to be more than that."

"E, you met up with Mason? Was he looking good as usual?" Shannon asked.

"We did not plan to meet up, but it happened, and, yes, he looks even better than he did two years ago," Eboni said while blushing.

Shannon shared her heart with Eboni and told her she might want to check and make sure that there is not another woman on his mind or in his life right now.

Eboni, on the other hand, did not really care, so she responded, "Shannon, if there was another woman, he would have said something about it, or he would have been eating lunch with her instead of me."

Before Shannon could say anything else, Eboni's next client came into the salon. She made a gesture to Shannon which signified that the conversation would continue later.

Shannon then left for her one-hour lunch break while Eboni started on her client.

Mason was now back at work, at Murphy's Investment Corporation. He was in his office in somewhat disbelief of what had just happened. Immediately, there was a knock on his door.

Looking up, he realized it was Danielle, so he told her she

could come in.

At a glance, she quickly knew something was wrong, so she inquired if he was okay.

"Yes. I just had lunch with an ex that I have not seen in about two years. She still thinks that we should be a couple."

"Okay, so, I am guessing that you don't think that you two should be a couple. Am I right, and if I am, why not? You don't have to answer if you think I am being too personal," Danielle said.

Mason was clear and sharp with his reply. "No, you are not being too personal. You see, five years ago I was to marry a certain young lady. Two weeks before the wedding we called it off because we believed then, and I still believe it today, that the Lord has someone else for us. Meaning we were meant to marry someone else. She asked me if I still have feelings for her, and I told her yes, only as a friend, but she insists on being more than that. I know what God told me, and I am sticking to that."

"Well, I know this, if that is what God told you to do at that time, then that is what you need to do, and I would throw some prayer on your ex because it seems like she might be getting a little bitter toward you and God." Danielle said.

Mason had enough of the Eboni talk, so he asked her about her lunch experience at the cafe.

"It was great. I met some more people that work in the building. This building has quite a variety of places to choose from to eat. I believe it should be renamed the "Variety Food Eatery.""

They both chuckled as he agreed. "Yeah, there are a variety of places to eat in the café. Just no Chick-fil-A. I think we need to change that," he said.

Danielle was only stopping by to look at the paperwork that was done for her next client, Mr. Anthony, and to find out what Mason thought about it. Mr. Barrett Anthony was one of Mason's favorite clients, and he assured Danielle that she too would love him. She was thrilled to hear that. She got her papers, went back to her office, and waited on Mr. Anthony.

Mason started looking at the paperwork he had for his next client.

Back at Danielle's desk, she was in disarray. She placed her hand on her forehead and asked, "Lord, what am I doing here? Is there a reason for this call? Please tell me because some things I do not understand. Lord, I pray this is not for Mason's benefit. Yes, he is fine and all, but you know Demond was enough for me. I do not want to go into another relationship too soon. Anyway, Lord, let Your will be done."

Soon enough, there was a knock at her door, and she knew for sure it was Mr. Anthony. He was an older client, but she was thrilled to work with him. She started her meeting assisting him with his investments. In the middle of the meeting, Danielle's office phone rang. It was Mason calling to check on her and to see if everything was going alright. She was doing ok and apologized to Mr. Anthony for the slight delay.

"Miss Danielle, are you married?" asked Mr. Anthony.

Danielle looked up at him and responded she was not.

Mr. Anthony was happily married to his wife for thirty-three years, so he was an advocate for healthy marriages. "I'm asking for my boy Mason across the hall. He is a really good fellow, and you seem to be a real good gal. He needs a good help mate, and you might be the one," said Mr. Anthony.

Danielle responded, "Sir, thank you but no thank you. I am not interested in Mr. Mason like that, and, yes, I see he is a good man in his words and actions. If the Lord sees fit for things to occur, then that is what will happen, but I am not asking for it."

"Alright, Miss Danielle, just keep your heart open and listen to God."

She responded she would and continued showing him the changes that she had made, the changes that were possible in his paperwork, and asking him questions about different things.

After her client left, Danielle called Mason on his office phone. "Mason, this is Danielle. Do you have a moment for me to come over and show you what I did concerning Mr. Anthony's investment plan and budget?"

"Sure, my client just left so come on over," he said.

In no time, Danielle knocked on Mason's office door.

"Come in," Mason said.

Danielle opened the door and sat down.

Mason was sure to apologize for causing an interruption between her and her client, Mr. Anthony. He just wanted to make sure she was okay and that things were running smoothly for her.

"Thank you for checking on me. Mr. Anthony is so nice and kind. He told me that the next time he comes to my office he is going to bring his wife, so I can meet her," Danielle said.

"Wow! That's great. You will enjoy their company. He started coming about five or six months after the company opened." Mason replied.

Having shared that, they started to examine what was discussed in her meeting earlier. "Well, this is what we discussed and went over," she said as she handed him the papers.

He looked them over and said, "This is exactly what I would have done. I guess our time together yesterday has us thinking alike. If this is what you were doing at your job before this one then, yes, you already know what to do and how to do it. I need to let Mr. Murphy know that you are a beast when it comes to these investment plans and budgets."

She thanked him for his compliment, expertise, and for helping her. Walking out of his office, she closed his door behind her, and when she was in the hallway alone, she looked up and said to herself, "Lord, You have to do this because I can't. Mason is too much of a perfect gentleman. Too good to be true. You are going to have to speak to me concerning him."

Meanwhile, back at the salon, Eboni and Shannon had clients under the dryer. Shannon continued the conversation about Eboni's lunch with Mason. "So, you met Mason at the Chick-fil-A downtown? What did he do? What did he say?"

Eboni answered, "Shannon, yes, he is still the finest man alive. Like I said, he knows that we are to be a couple. He acted like a perfect gentleman as usual. He never got loud with me, either. He made me want to be his woman all over again. You know how he likes to be neatly dressed. Every time he stood up, he made sure his pants, belt and tie were right. We talked for a moment while we ate. Then after we finished eating, he threw the trash away and helped me up from the table and we went our separate ways. I still love him, Shannon, and I must help him to love me back like I love him."

"E, you can't make a man love you. If he loves you, he loves you. If he does not love you, he does not love you. It is what it is. I am glad you had a chance to see him. My question still is, what if he has another woman that he is interested in?"

"Shannon, you know what, even if he does have another woman he is interested in, his interest is about to change," Eboni said.

"Okay, E, if that is what you are doing. Just be careful because you know doing things like that has a way of backfiring on you."

"Girl, I have God on my side, and I believe this is His will," Eboni said.

Shannon's last words of warning were for Eboni to be careful. They both went back to check on their clients and to finish their hair.

When a few hours passed, Eboni was with her last client of the day. As she placed her under the dryer, she looked up and told the Lord thank you. She was happy to be almost finished for the day.

Shannon came over again to ask about Mason and what the

next plans were to see him. After so many years, Mason still had the same number, which made it easy for Eboni to get back in touch with him.

Out of curiosity, Shannon asked, "Does he have a brother, or was it just him and his sister? I forget."

"It's just him and his sister. Now, he does have some guy friends that aren't shabby either. All three of them used to work out together. I'm not sure if they still do. His two friends are Quintin and Jason. I forget their last names, but they are very kind, and they all have similar personalities," Eboni told Shannon.

"Well, girl, I need to get out of here so that I can make it to the gym today. I will see you in the morning."

Eboni cleaned up her space and left because she knew she had an early morning tomorrow, and she was going to also leave early, around two or three in the afternoon.

Later that day, at Murphy's Investment Corporation, Mason was packing up to go home, and he jokingly asked Danielle if she needed an escort today.

"No. I am alright, and I have some more paperwork I want to look over and some that I need to take home to look over," Danielle responded.

He said okay and that he would see her tomorrow and left.

While walking to his car, he said, "Lord, I thank You for Danielle, and I pray Your continued blessings around her."

When he was finally home, he changed into his gym clothes to meet Quintin and Jason at the track two miles from his house. When he got there, he saw Quintin and Jason warming up their muscles. He got out of his car and ran over to join them.

They started their five-mile run around the track. Two miles into it, Jason noticed that Mason was not in his zone like he normally would be. They kept on running as Jason said to himself that it would be better to ask Mason about it when they were done.

When they were finished and cooling down, Jason asked, "Mason, are you alright? Because you were not in your zone during the laps. Seems like you were more focused on something else."

That's when Mason started to talk about his day. "Guys, I'm sorry. I ran into Eboni today while I was having lunch at the Chick-fil-A downtown. I had lunch with her. She was talking about being more than friends, and I know that is not going to work and I told her that. We did finish our lunch together, and when we were leaving, you know I had to hold the door for her, that's when she felt it was cool to rub herself up against me."

Quintin could not believe Mason was refusing Eboni because from what he remembered she had an amazing body like no other.

Jason however had contradicting thoughts "Mason, I am thankful that you are standing for what you believe God said to you. It helps me to be more obedient to Him and a better husband to my wife."

He thanked them and explained he just wanted to obey God and get the best that He has for him.

"Man, I am with you on that," said Jason.

"Man, I'm sorry, but she was fine," Quintin said.

Mason invited them over to have a post workout smoothie at his house, so they left the track and were in route to Mason's crib. It seemed like forever since Jason and Quintin had been over to Mason's house, so they were amazed at how he had reorganized the living spaces to include a bigger man cave.

In the kitchen, Mason got out the fresh fruit he bought from the grocery store yesterday. He washed them off and started the process of making the smoothie. He added everything to the blender, including some ice and unsweetened vanilla-flavored milk. He also added a little protein powder. The smoothie was a hit! Both guys enjoyed every ounce of it.

"I do these smoothies every time I come home from the gym, then I eat a salad. That keeps me until the next morning. Come on to the back so I can show you two my man cave," Mason said.

They went to the back of his house off from the kitchen. Jason was surprised to see how what the patio was once was now a huge man cave.

"This was the patio. I just had it closed in, these windows put in, and this nice little electrical fireplace put in. Do you like it?" asked Mason.

Quintin looked around, went and sat on the couch, and said, "I like it, man. This is the bomb. Mason, I want to be like you when I grow up."

Mason threw a couch pillow at him.

They sat and talked for an hour. As the night came, the gentlemen decided it was time to head home. "Alright, brothers. I will see you two tomorrow at the gym," said Mason.

After they left, Mason cleaned up the kitchen and with a grateful heart he said, "God, I thank You for my friends who have become brothers to me. Thank you, Lord, that they help me to stay grounded and to stay focused on You and Your word." Feeling pleased, he went to take a shower.

Since it was only eight o' clock, he decided to see what was showing on the television. While he was relaxing, his phone rang. He looked at the caller ID and saw that it was his dad. "Good evening, Dad. How are you?" he answered.

"Good evening, Son. I am doing well. I was praying concerning you, and the Lord showed me two women. One is going to try to wreak havoc, and one you will marry. I don't mean to get your spirit out of sorts, but I called to tell you to be even more prayerful and you might want to start doing some fasting here and there," said his dad.

"Wow, Dad, thanks for calling me and letting me know what God is saying to you concerning me. I greatly appreciate it, and I will get to praying about that now," Mason said.

Feeling compelled to pray, his father prayed over him right at that moment. "Father in heaven, we humbly come before Your throne of grace. We are thankful for how You kept us throughout this day. We are also thankful for how You will keep us through the night. Lord, I ask Your continual blessings upon my son. Continue to make Your face shine upon him. Continue to grace him with Your anointing. Lord, whatever is not like You that is in him, bring it to his spirit so it can come out. Lord, I pray right now that You will grant him the wisdom, he needs for what You have shown me concerning him. I bind all the attacks of the enemy and call them to naught. Lord be glorified in and through his life in

Your son Christ Jesus' name. Amen. Son, I will talk to you tomorrow. Have a good night."

Mason responded, "You have a good night too, Dad, and I will talk to you tomorrow also."

The call ended, but Mason was still a little perplexed, so he got on his knees and began to pray. "Lord, I love You. Lord, I need You to take care of this problem because I cannot do it. Lord, I need You to do it. I trust You, and I thank You for working this out on my behalf in advance. Amen."

He then snuggled up and fell asleep.

At Danielle's house, she was preparing to go to bed. She prayed, "Lord, what are You doing in this season with me? You know that I did not want this job because of Mason. I did not even know him until I was hired, and he trained me to do what I am doing now. Lord, if You want us to have this 'more than friends' relationship then You will have to do what needs to be done for that to happen. I cannot do what needs to be done without You. If this is Your will for Mason and me, please help me in this season of my life. I also pray for Mason. I pray that You continue to grant him favor and wisdom for the things and people that are coming his way. Lord, I thank You for answering my prayer in Jesus' name, amen."

Meanwhile, Eboni sipped on her green tea while trying to figure out how she can meet up with Mason again. She said to herself, "Maybe I can go to his job, and maybe we can have lunch there. That is what I will do." She finished her tea, prayed, and went to bed.

CHAPTER 6:
The Prayers That Avail Much

The next morning, Mason woke up at three, and his first thought was the conversation he had with his dad before bed last night. He then started to pray. Mason travailed in prayer until around five that morning. "Oh Lord, I want to pray the prayers that avail much."

When he was finished, he was drenched, and his clothes were wet. He got up, took his shower, and fixed some oatmeal to eat for breakfast along with some grapes and a cup of orange juice.

While having breakfast, he did his devotional before getting ready for work.

In no time, Mason was on his way to work when he saw a car race past him followed by several police cars giving chase. Mason drove onto the shoulder of the street to get out of the way. Then he prayed for the policemen and the person driving the car they were chasing.

When he got around the curve to continue on to work, he saw that the policemen did stop the car and apprehend the person who was driving. Driving over the bridge, he was so thankful for the water and how beautiful it looked in the morning. He drove on to work.

Across town, Eboni was up early. She turned on her coffee pot and went to get a shower. After her shower, she went back to her kitchen and fixed some cheese grits and bacon for her to eat for breakfast, enjoying the quietness of the morning.

When she was ready, Eboni headed to the salon. She was thinking about how many clients she would have and who was working at the salon today. She also thought about going to Mason's job to have lunch with him. How lovely that would be. She made sure to put a change of clothes in a bag that she believed he would like to see her in. She considered changing before she went to his job.

When she got to the salon, she saw Shannon's car and four other cars.

She parked her car and went in.

After saying good morning, Shannon spotted the bag and asked, "Are you going out of town?" to which Eboni explained her elaborate plan to go see Mason unannounced for lunch.

"Are you sure that is a good idea?" asked Shannon.

"It is the best idea. He needs to know that I am still available and that we can still be together," said Eboni.

"Alright, if you say so," Shannon said.

Eboni took her things to the back and then got things ready for her first client.

Ten blocks from Mason's house, Danielle was home praying since five that morning. She was sweaty from head to toe. She got up and went to get her shower and prepared her breakfast.

While she sat enjoying her oatmeal, bacon, strawberries, and a cup of coffee, she felt it was the opportune time to do her devotional reading.

Once she was ready for work, she whispered a little prayer before going through the doors. "Lord, I do want Your will to be done, but, Lord, You have to get me ready for the will You have for me. I know that Mason is the husband You have for me. Lord, I need You to get me ready for him. Amen."

She was now ready to go see what her week would bring.

When she got to work, she saw that Mason was already there. Even after being friends for a while, she still got nervous in his presence.

She walked into the building, and the first person she saw was Mason going up the elevator. He greeted and checked on her because, to him, she seemed to be having a rough morning, and he wanted to make sure she was okay.

He then walked into his office and assessed his workload on his desk and said, "Lord, I need Your help with this. I cannot do this without You." He got up from his desk and went to Danielle's office door and knocked.

"Come in," she said.

Mason walked through the door, and Danielle froze.

"Are you alright?" asked Mason.

"Ummm, yes, I am. I just have some extra things on my mind today," Danielle responded.

"Would you be willing to talk about it over some lunch? I can at least listen and pray," Mason said.

"Sure. Maybe it will help me out. What time would be good for you?" she asked.

They agreed at one o'clock, and Mason went back to his office.

Back at the salon, Shannon was curious to know what exactly Eboni was getting herself into, thinking it was ok to pop up at Mason's job.

"I will go change around eleven-fifteen and leave between eleven-thirty and eleven forty-five. That way I can make it to his job by twelve noon for our lunch date."

"E, you know this is very interesting to me, especially the fact that you are going on a lunch date with Mason. I hope it goes well," said Shannon.

"Shannon, today I will be with the love of my life, and he will enjoy our time together," Eboni said.

"Girl, I wish I could be a fly on the wall. Please, you must tell me all the happenings when you get back. What time is your next client supposed to be here anyway?" Shannon asked.

Eboni responded, "Shannon, you know that I will let you know about all the happenings, and my next client is due to be here at two this afternoon."

"Well, I hope things go the way you desire them to during lunch with the love of your life," Shannon said.

"Thanks, Shannon. I believe things will go the way I desire them to go." She finished up her client's hair while she ended her chat.

Back at Murphy's Investment Corporation, there was a knock-on Mason's office door. It was Danielle needing help. She was looking through Mr. Anthony's paperwork again and felt she missed something. She showed Mason the paperwork, and he looked it over.

He asked, "Can you show me what you are talking about?"

She answered, "It is highlighted in the pink."

"Oh, okay. I see what you are talking about. Well, you can fix that by changing this around and adding this," he said. He passed her the papers back and showed her the changes he made.

"Thanks, Mason. I appreciate it," said Danielle.

"You are welcome. Are we still on for one this afternoon?" asked Mason.

"Yes, we are," said Danielle as she walked out of his office door. She closed the door behind her, and Mason went back to look at his client's paperwork.

While at the salon, Eboni got dressed and asked Shannon what she thought. "So, Shannon, how do I look?" Eboni asked.

"Girl, you look great. He will definitely want to get back with you," said Shannon.

"Thanks, Shannon. I have to go now so I will not be late."

"Alright. Have a good time," said Shannon to Eboni as she walked out the door.

As she drove across town, Eboni said, "Lord, I believe this is Your will for me and Mason. Please let him be open-minded." She continued to drive until she got to Mason's job and saw an empty parking spot right beside his car.

She parked, got out of her car, and went to ring the doorbell so that someone at the front desk would let her in. She told the young lady at the front door that she had an appointment with Mr. Mason Taylor.

The young lady told her to get on the elevator and to go up to the third floor, and she gave Eboni his office number, 312.

"Thank you," said Eboni as she walked to the elevator.

When she got to his office door, she knocked. She heard a voice on the other side of the door telling her to come in. She opened the door and entered the room.

Across the hallway, Danielle was working on the paperwork of another client. She got to a spot where she was not sure if she needed to place this client's funds in a certain area to invest or not so she said to herself, "Mason would know how to budget these funds and where to place them better than I would. I don't know why my focus is so off right now."

She grabbed the paperwork and got up from her desk. By Mason's door, she heard him talking to someone, but it did not sound like a client, so she knocked on his office door.

"Come in," she heard Mason say.

As she entered, she saw him standing next to a gorgeous young lady. "Mason, I see that you are busy here. I can come back later. Sorry to interrupt," Danielle said.

Mason looked at her and said, "No, Danielle. It is okay. This is Eboni Cutler, an old family friend. Eboni, this is Danielle Belkin. She works in the office across the hallway from me."

"Nice to meet you," Danielle said to Eboni while holding her hand out for a handshake.

Eboni shook her hand and said, "It is nice to meet you too, Mrs. Danielle."

"It's just Miss. I am not married," she said.

"Oh, okay. I am an old friend of the family, and I will be back for a visit sometime next week. It is always a pleasure seeing you, Mason. I will let you get back to your work," Eboni said as she walked out of Mason's office door.

"Thank you for coming, Eboni," said Mason.

"Mason, is everything okay in here?" asked Danielle.

"All is well, Danielle. Eboni came for lunch, but I know I told you earlier that I will be having lunch with you so that we can talk about some things."

"Mason, if she is an old family friend, you could have had lunch with her. I did not mean to stop what you two had going on."

Mason looked at her and said, "Danielle, you were not interrupting anything. She wanted to catch up on some things that I want to put behind me. What did you need? I see the papers in your hand."

"Oh, yes. I've been thinking about so many other things lately that I am not able to focus enough to do what all needs to be done with this client's paperwork," said Danielle.

"Well, let me take a look," Mason said.

Meanwhile, at the elevator, Eboni said to herself, "Wow, Danielle is beautiful. I wonder if Mason is into her. Nah, she's not Mason's type. I'm his type, and I will be back to let him know that. Old family friend, ha."

The elevator came to a stop. She got out, spoke to the young lady at the front and left out of the building.

"I cannot believe Mason turned down a lunch date with me. I hope he is not trying to talk to that Miss Danielle because that is not going to work."

She drove to Chick-fil-A where she sat inside and had lunch solo.

Back at the investment company, Mason finished the paperwork he was working on. He placed it on the table, grabbed his keys, and left out his office door. Across the hallway, he knocked on Danielle's office door.

"Are you ready?" asked Mason.

"Yes. Just give me a moment. I need to put this information in the system really quickly," Danielle said.

"Okay," said Mason as he sat and waited. "Have you thought about where you want to eat? I've thought of a few places, but I want to be respectful and allow the lady to go first." Mason said.

"That's done, and yes, I have thought about some lunch places. Will it be okay if we went somewhere away from the job?" Danielle asked.

Mason responded, "You know, that sounds great. It might be good for the both of us."

She picked up her purse, and they walked to the door. They talked about where they could eat while they walked to the elevator. Danielle had a taste for some seafood, so Mason knew the right place to take her. He took her downtown to Rob's Seafood and More.

The weekend after the lunch date, Temperance, her husband Mario, and their three girls came to visit Mason. As usual, Mason had some fun activities planned for the family. That Saturday morning, they rode for an hour to get to an amusement park. After the amusement park, they had a picnic lunch in a park. The girls enjoyed this because after they ate, they were able to play for a while. They walked around in the park for about thirty minutes.

After the park, Mason had a one-gift surprise for them, so they went to the mall. Everyone enjoyed their one gift.

On the way home, the girls fell asleep.

Temperance asked, "So, Mason, it has been a while, but have you talked to God, or has he shown You my sister yet? That is, the young lady you will marry?"

"The answer to that question is yes, and you will get a chance to meet her soon," said Mason.

"Yay! What's her name?" Temperance asked.

Mason answered, "Her name is Danielle Belkin, and she works across the hallway from me."

"That is great, Mason. We are happy for you," said Temperance and Mario. "We will wait patiently to meet her," Temperance said.

They made it back to Mason's house. Temperance told the girls to get their pajamas and get ready for their baths.

As the girls were getting their baths, Temperance fixed dinner while Mason and Mario chilled in the man cave. She cooked her famous fried chicken wings that she has a special seasoning for, collard greens with smoked neck bones, and candied yams with sweet tea.

Everyone sat in the formal dining room to eat since there was more space there. After everyone was seated, Mason blessed the food, and they ate it all.

"Sis, thank you for cooking dinner. It tastes almost like mom did it," Mason said.

"Now you see why she is my wife, and I have to do her good," said Mario.

They cleaned up the kitchen, and everyone got ready for bed so they could be up and ready for church tomorrow.

The lunch date Mason and Danielle had earlier that week started a six-month time of them getting to know one another. Eboni did come to see Mason again, but he was out of his office at the time, so she was thinking about how she would meet up with him again. Mason told Danielle about his relationship with his old family friend, Eboni Cutler, and Danielle got to meet Mason's parents and sibling. Mason also met Danielle's parents and siblings too.

SIX MONTHS LATER

CHAPTER 7:
When The Devil Comes To Steal

On a Saturday evening in March, Mason invited his parents, sibling, Danielle, her parents, her siblings, and their family, as well as some of their friends for what Danielle thought was a cookout. Everyone was talking, laughing, eating, and drinking.

Mason excused himself for a moment. He went into his house down the hallway to his bedroom. He looked in his t-shirt drawer and took out this little box. When he turned around to leave his room, his dad was standing at the door. Mason was startled.

"I just came to check on you and make sure you were okay, Son. I know this has been and is getting ready to be a big day for you; you are making me and your mother happy. Now, go make Danielle happy," Mr. Taylor said.

He hugged his dad, and they left the room and went back to his backyard together.

Everyone was still having a good time.

Mason blew a whistle to get everyone's attention. "Good evening, everyone. Thank you all so much for coming to this cookout. I am also very thankful that the Lord allowed the day to be very lovely and beautiful. Danielle, will you come beside me, please?" Mason said.

Danielle came to stand beside him with a bewildered look on her face.

Mason grabbed Danielle's hand, he looked at her, and said, "Danielle, the past six months have been life for me. Getting to know you and your family has been a Godsend. Danielle, you help complete me, and I want our relationship to continue on into something more." He got on one knee and pulled the box off the table beside his chair and said as he opened the box, "Danielle, will you marry me?"

Danielle was taken aback. She answered with tears rolling down her face, "Mason, I would be honored to marry you."

They hugged, and he kissed her on her forehead. Two weeks later they started marital counseling.

Mason's family and Temperance's three girls loved them some Danielle. Their names were Olivia, Nevaeh, and Jasmine. They started calling her auntie a few times after they met her. They were very excited when Mason proposed to Danielle because they knew that they would be involved in the wedding. Danielle's best friends Joi' and Syncere were not able to be there, but the first time they met Mason, they told Danielle that he was the one for her.

Danielle thanked God for her best friends daily.

As time went by, Mason and Danielle really got to know each other more during their counseling sessions. Their counseling sessions were done by a Pastor that Mason and Danielle's parents knew and were friends with. They had two to three-hour sessions once a week.

Mason and Danielle set their wedding date for December thirtieth. They spoke to their families, and everyone agreed they would make themselves available for that time.

One day at the gym, Mason was talking with Quintin and Jason. "Wow, this year is going by so fast. It is so amazing how God is working things out for me and Danielle. I am so thankful. I am thankful for you two and for the encouragement you have given me," Mason said.

"Mason, man, you deserve it. I see the way Danielle looks at you and the way you look at her. God is all in that. You have to give Him His props," Quintin said.

"Let's finish this workout because I have a date with Danielle tonight," said Mason.

"Yes, because you do not want to have milady waiting," said Jason. All three laughed, and Quintin and Mason threw a towel at Jason.

They finished their workout.

Across town, Eboni didn't know that Mason had asked Danielle to marry him. In her mind, they just worked across the hallway from each another, and they had nothing in common other than their work. Eboni wanted to meet up with Mason again in the next week, so she set up a plan to meet up with him.

Later on, that evening, Mason, and Danielle went to Rosmano, an Italian restaurant. They both had a taste for something Italian. While eating and talking, Mason received a phone call. He didn't recognize the number, so he dismissed the call, which sent the person to his voicemail. He and Danielle continued their conversation.

Again, his phone vibrated, and it was the same number.

Danielle said, "Mason, maybe you should answer it, just to make sure nothing is going on that you need to know about."

Mason answered the call.

"Hi, my love," said the voice on the other end of the phone.

Mason thought about who it could be. He said, "I am not able to talk right now. Can I call you back later?"

"Mason, I love you, and I know you love me. Let's just meet tomorrow for lunch. One o'clock tomorrow afternoon. I will see you then," said Eboni. She hung up before he was able to say anything.

"Mason, dear, is everything okay?" asked Danielle.

"Yes, sweetheart, everything is okay."

They continued to talk and eat.

After they left the restaurant, Mason took Danielle home. He walked her to her front door. Once she opened the door, he kissed her on her forehead and told her that he loved her, and he went back to his vehicle.

She told him to call her when he makes it home.

When he got home, he noticed that his front door looked like it was cracked.

He parked his car and went up to the door to check, and, sure enough, his door had popped open. He pushed the door open only to hear glass shattering from his kitchen area.

He ran into his kitchen just in time to see a person in all black running through his back yard and jumping over the fence. Mason said to himself, "So, this is when the devil comes to steal, after a blessed time with my fiancée?"

He called the police, and within minutes, they were on the

scene. The chief introduced himself as Officer Broyles.

He also called his parents and Danielle to let them know what happened.

While he was talking to Officer Broyles, his parents drove up, and after them, Danielle came.

Officer Broyles looked up with his hand on his gun.

"Officer these are my parents, and that is my fiancée with them," Mason said.

Danielle came to his side with tears in her eyes.

Mason looked at her and said, "Sweetheart, what's wrong? I am okay, and I don't believe he stole anything. I am okay, sweetheart."

They walked with Officer Broyles into the house. As they were looking, Mason realized they were trying to steal his television, gaming consoles, and remotes because they were boxed up.

They got to the kitchen, and that was where they saw that whoever the person was had broken the glass on Mason's back door.

Danielle looked at Mason and said, "Honey, will you go to a hotel tonight until you get your doors fixed? I know you will be able to get them fixed tomorrow."

Mason responded, "Yes, I will do that to keep your spirit at ease, but I am upset about this because I work hard for everything that I have. God blesses me to work."

The Officer finished his walk through the house, did the police report, and gave Mason a card with the police report number on it. He also left his information with Mason.

Mason and his dad tacked plastic on the window of the back door, and they boarded up the front door area.

Afterwards, Mason packed a few items for the hotel stay. He walked Danielle to her car, making sure she was okay. Assuring her he was okay, he promised to call as soon as he got into the room. He opened the car door for her, kissed her forehead, and told her he loved her before she drove away.

His parents stayed as they continued to cover the broken doors. They were thankful that no windows were smashed. Instead of going to a hotel, Mason went to his parents' house. He left his car parked in his driveway and rode in the car with his parents.

Once he got to their house, he went to his childhood room, where he settled and called Danielle. "Sweetheart, I am at my parent's home. After you left, we talked for a moment so, they said I could stay the night at their house and save the money I would spend staying at a hotel."

"Honey, that is great. I am glad that you are okay and safe," Danielle said.

"I am, sweetie. Now we both need to get some rest, and I will talk with you tomorrow," said Mason.

They hung up, and Mason prayed and went to sleep.

The next morning, Mason was up early making calls to his insurance company and contractors to work on his house. He made all the connections he needed to make for the repairs to be done that day. Then he left for work. He made frequent calls from work to confirm everything got done.

SIX MONTHS LATER

CHAPTER 8:
Wow! It's Really Happening

Danielle was getting ready for her girls' night. She got out of bed and went into prayer. "Lord, I thank You for being so good to Mason and me. We know that You are in our relationship through and through. I pray that You will continue to walk us through this journey of engagement and into marriage. Now, Lord, guide my footsteps on today. Grant me the strength I need for this girl's night. Thank you in advance. Amen."

She got up, showered, and left to run her errands for the day. It was a Friday, and they both took this day off for wedding purposes and their events.

Meanwhile, Mason was up and super thrilled about the bachelor party his dad and friends were throwing for him. "God, I thank You for all things," Mason screamed in his bedroom. "Wow, only a few more months and I will marry the woman of my dreams! Wow! It's really happening! God, I thank You! This is going to be one of the best days ever! I am so grateful and humbled when I think about all that You have done. Bless, keep, and strengthen Danielle in whatever she has going on today. Lord, You are worthy of all glory, honor, and praise. I thank You for answering my prayers in advance. Amen."

He got up from his knees and started getting things ready for a one-night hotel stay. He and Danielle had planned to have lunch together, so he left his house to run some errands quickly.

Later that afternoon, they met up for lunch. They discussed their plans for that evening and more of their expectations for one another.

After lunch was over, they went their separate ways to handle more errands. Danielle went to the airport to pick up her parents who would be in town for the weekend. Her two sisters, and their families were already at hotels for the weekend. Her sister, Sonya, had a daughter who was seventeen and very responsible. She would be watching her little sisters and her cousins while her mom, aunt, and uncles attended the planned events.

"Mom, I know you had some other obligations for this evening, but I am so happy you were able to come for this weekend," Danielle said to her mom.

"Honey, I enjoy spending time with you. Any obligation can wait. Now, let's get to your house so I can get settled and your dad can go with your fiancé and his dad."

That evening at Danielle's house, she was talking with her mother about her ex-fiancé, while they waited for the other ladies to arrive.

"Well, I just want to let you know how pleased I am with you. You listened to me somewhat when I told you what the Lord showed me concerning Demond. Now He has brought someone else into your life that is going to treat you like a queen. You deserve it sweetheart. I love you," said her mother.

"I love you, too, Mom," said Danielle.

Danielle's doorbell rang. She went to open the door, and it was Mrs. Taylor, Mason's mother.

"Good evening, Mama Taylor. I am so glad that you could make it this evening. My sisters and my other friends will be here a little later. Let's get this party started," said Danielle.

She popped the popcorn with her mom's help, and she already had a movie set for them to start off with.

They brought the popcorn to the living room and ate as they watched *Fireproof*. After the movie, they discussed the things that happened, The things they enjoyed and the things they did not enjoy as much.

After their discussion, Danielle asked, "Who's ready for the next movie?"

"We are," said Mrs. Taylor and her mom in unison.

The doorbell rang again. Danielle went and answered the door. It was Joi’ and Syncere. They came in and gave Danielle a hug.

“Hey, guys, I have someone here I want you to meet. This is my mom as you two know,” said Danielle.

“Hi, Mrs. Belkin.” Joi and Syncere said as they gave her a hug.

Danielle then looked to her left. “This is Mason’s mom, Mrs. Taylor.”

Joi’ and Syncere said their hellos and gave her a hug and let her know that it was great to meet her.

Syncere looked at Danielle and asked, “Have you all seen *War Room* yet?”

Danielle answered, “Not yet, but it is on the list.”

Joi’ looked all wide-eyed and asked, “You have a list?”

“Yes, I have a list. This is girls’ night. No men allowed. Remember, you two are staying the night here,” said Danielle.

Joi’ looked at Syncere and answered, “Yes, I remember. Let us get our bags out of the car.” They went to Joi’s car and got their bags.

While they were getting their bags out of the car, Sonya and Cicely drove up. They got out and got their bags out of the trunk of the rental car they were in.

When they came back into the living room, Danielle greeted everyone, introduced them to one another, and showed them where they would be sleeping so they could put their bags down.

Mrs. Belkin was finishing up some popcorn for everyone. After she gave them their bowl of popcorn, she looked at Danielle and asked, "Danielle, what is *War Room* about?"

"Mom, if I tell you what it is about, I will have to tell you the movie," answered Danielle.

"Well, can we watch *War Room* now because I believe we all have seen the *Left Behind* series?" asked Syncere.

Everyone looked at Danielle and nodded their heads yes.

"Sure, we can watch it next. I think you will enjoy it," Danielle said.

Meanwhile, the guys had finished their bowling and were out at Chili's getting ready to eat.

"Dad, I feel like I have butterflies on the inside. I feel excited and nervous at the same time," said Mason.

"Son, that sounds normal. In a few months, you will be marrying a beautiful young lady, who is a godly young lady. No, it will not be a bed of roses all the time, and it will not be a pot of poop all the time either. Always keep God first and foremost in all things. Always allow time to hear from Him in every situation and circumstance. Never allow the devil to have any space because he hates marriages," said Mr. Taylor.

"Ron, may I add something, please?" Mr. Belkin asked.

"Yes sir, doc," answered Mr. Taylor.

"Mason, I see you and Danielle as blessings to each other. I believe you have been and are a blessing to your parents, and Danielle has been and is a blessing to her mother and me. I will be glad to become your second dad and not your in-law because sometimes in-laws can become out-laws, if you know what I mean," said Mr. Belkin.

Mason, with tears in his eyes, said, "I thank God for the both of you. I cannot express enough of how grateful I am to God for you two. I am thankful for how my dad has taught and trained me to be a man and for the way both of you helped me to be and stay accountable. I know that Danielle is the mate God ordained for me to have. When I first met her, I heard the Lord say, "This is your bride." I know that every day will not be cake and ice cream, but with God, He will make all things work."

"Son, He is making it work right now. Let us pray."

They all grabbed each other's hands and prayed.

Back at Danielle's house, the women just ended their prayer. Everyone was teary-eyed and excited about a wedding that would be happening in a couple of months.

"Everyone, we have two more counseling sessions to go to. I am always excited and nervous to be in the sessions because we never know what will happen and how God will move," Danielle said.

"Danielle, you are Mason's prized possession. Other than God, you are most of what he talks about. I am glad God sent you to him. I am blessed to have another daughter."

By this time, Danielle was bawling.

"What's wrong, dear?" her mother asked.

She wiped her eyes, cheeks, and answered, "Before I met Mason, I always dreamed of the Lord blessing me with a godly husband. I didn't know what God was up to the day Mason and I met. I just remember the Lord saying to me, "Get ready because this is your husband." I looked up, and I was like, God, he looks too good for me, and are you for real? That was not the only time He showed me that Mason was my husband. There were two other times. When I accepted him, that's when God started allowing things to go forward. I did not know how you would accept me, Mama Taylor, or how Papa Taylor and Temperance would accept me. Now I am so overwhelmed with how the Lord has blessed me with another set of parents and another sister. I am tremendously, abundantly blessed."

When she finished talking, all the ladies hugged.

Temperance, Joi', and Syncere got ready to go to their room where they would sleep. Danielle, Sonya, and Cicely went to their room where they would sleep also. Mrs. Belkin and Mrs. Taylor shared Danielle's master bedroom.

"Good night, everyone. See you in the morning" they said.

Danielle said good night to her mother and Mrs. Taylor. They all went to bed.

CHAPTER 9:

No Weapon Formed Shall Prosper I

Early the next morning, Danielle got out of bed and prayed about the day and that all will go well at her bridal shower and for Mason and his party.

After praying, she knew she smelled bacon in the air.

Trying not to wake her guests, she walked down to the kitchen where she heard her mother and Mrs. Taylor talking. She stopped in her tracks to just listen to their conversation.

"This is going to be the best bridal shower I have ever been to. Did Temperance tell you about the games and surprises?" Mrs. Belkin asked Mrs. Taylor.

"Yes, I told her Danielle was going to be surprised, and she was going to enjoy herself as well as her sisters and her friends."

By this time, everyone was awake and heading to the kitchen.

"Good morning, bride-to-be."

She smiled at them, and they walked into the kitchen one behind the other.

"Good morning, ladies," said Mrs. Belkin and Mrs. Taylor.

"Good morning," said Danielle, Temperance, Joi', Syncere, Sonya, and Cicely.

"It smells like the Cracker Barrel in here. What have you two cooked?" asked Temperance.

"We did not mean to wake you ladies. We just wanted to do something together in the kitchen. We have oatmeal, cereal, and milk if anyone is hungry. We also have bacon, scrambled and boiled eggs, sausage, pancakes, waffles, and brats," said Mrs. Belkin.

"This is a lot of food for just the eight of us," Syncere said.

"It's not only for us. Your dad, Pastor Ron, Mason, Quintin, Jason, Mario, Craig, and Dillan will be here in about fifteen minutes." Danielle's mother responded.

"Well, we are going to go back in the room and get dressed before we eat," Danielle said. They left the kitchen to go get dressed.

While the girls were going to their room to get dressed, the doorbell rang.

Mrs. Belkin answered the door. "Good morning. How may I

help you?”

“Yes ma’am. My name is Eboni Cutler, and I really need to talk to Danielle,” the strange lady at the door said.

Mrs. Belkin reluctantly said, “Okay, give me a moment. I will go get her for you. Come on in.” Mrs. Belkin went to go snatch Danielle from the guest bedroom to let her know she had company.

“Danielle, Eboni Cutler is here to see you,” said Mrs. Belkin.

“Alright, I will be there in a moment. I just need to put these shoes on.”

“Danielle, who is this Eboni person?” asked Sonya.

“She is Mason’s ex-fiancée. I don’t know how she got my address,” Danielle answered.

“Well, let’s go see what she wants,” Sonya said.

On the way back to the living room, Mrs. Belkin heard Mrs. Taylor talking to the young lady. “Eboni, how are you? It has been a few years since I have seen you.”

“I am good. I just need to talk to Danielle,” Eboni explained.

Mrs. Belkin walked back into the living room and let her know Danielle would be out in a moment.

"So, Sylvia, you know this young lady?"

Mrs. Taylor answered, "Yes, her and Mason were engaged to be married about five years ago, but they believed that they were not the one for each other."

Eboni quickly responded, "Well, that is what Mason said. He knows that we are still getting married, and this is not right, what he is doing to this girl, Danielle."

"What!" exclaimed Mrs. Taylor and Mrs. Belkin.

Danielle walked into the living room along with Sonya and Cicely. "Hi, Eboni. How may I help you?" Danielle asked.

"Danielle, you know Mason is my husband?"

"Eboni, I don't know what you are talking about, but you need to leave," Danielle exclaimed. As she opened the door for Eboni to leave, in walked the rest of the family, including Mr. Ron Taylor, Mr. Belkin, Mason, Quintin, Jason, Craig, and Dillan.

Before they could speak, Eboni walked over to Mason and forcefully tried to kiss him on the lips. He pushed her off and asked her what her problem was.

Eboni answered, "You know what the problem is. We are still getting married, and you are playing around with Danielle's feelings."

"What are you talking about? Never mind. Is it okay if I walk her out? Please excuse us," Mason said angrily.

He grabbed her arm to walk her out, then she turned, looked at Danielle with a weird grin and said, "See? I told you."

When they got outside, Mason asked, "Eboni, why did you come here to cause problems, and how did you get Danielle's address anyway?"

She answered, "Mason, you know we are the ones that should be getting married and living happily ever after. Why are you faking with this girl, Danielle? Yeah, she might be cute, but you know she cannot give you what I can."

"Well, listen, can we talk about this later, please?" Mason asked.

"Yes, we can deal with this later, but I will not wait long," she said. She got in her truck and left.

Back inside the house, Mason apologized to everyone. "I am so sorry about that Dad, Mom, and Mr. and Mrs. Belkin. Where is Danielle?" he asked.

"Son, we have to get some things straight."

"I know, Dad, but where is Danielle?"

Mrs. Belkin answered, "She is in her guest bedroom with her sisters and friends. That is where her and the other young ladies slept last night."

He stormed out of the living room to the guest bedroom. He knocked and asked to speak with Danielle in private. "Ladies, may I please talk to Danielle privately for a moment, please?"

They glanced at Danielle to see if she wanted them to leave. She looked at them and said, "It is okay. I trust Mason."

Temperance was the last to walk out. She gave him that disappointed sister look and closed the door behind her as she walked out.

"Mason, why did Eboni come here to my house, and how did she get my address?"

"I don't know how she got your address. You know our past. After what just happened, I believe I still have some things that I need to straighten out," said Mason.

"Do you still have feelings for her?"

"No. I do not," he replied.

"Okay. If that is so, why is she coming around now talking about you two getting married and all? Do we need to cancel the bridal shower and your bachelor party until this is taken care of?"

He answered, "No. Danielle, I will get this taken care of. I will not let the devil win this fight. Can we have breakfast, please, and if you want, we can continue this conversation with our parents."

She said, "I really do not want to talk about it because for me it is embarrassing. She came to my home and tried to kiss my fiancé, my future protector and provider and thinks that it is fine. Mason, it is not. She did this in front of our parents."

"Danielle baby, I love you, and I desire to spend the rest of my life with you. You are the woman God showed me will be my wife. I love the Lord too much to allow the devil to come in and just take what he wants."

"Mason, if you are being truthful with me right now, I am willing to fight with you," she said.

"Well, with that being said, can we pray about it now?"

She replied yes, and they held hands and prayed.

After they prayed, Mason looked Danielle in the eyes and said, "No weapon formed will prosper." He then kissed her on her forehead.

Meanwhile in Danielle's kitchen, their parents were having a conversation. "Ron, I thought Mason and Eboni said that they did not believe the Lord put them together. They were not the one for each other?" Mrs. Taylor asked her husband.

"That was what they said, and that is what Mason told me last week when we were talking about some things," answered Mr. Taylor.

"So, what is going on? Who was that lady? You two know her?" asked Mr. Belkin.

Mr. Taylor answered, "Eboni is a young lady that Mason was engaged to five years ago. During their time of counseling with Pastor Andy Rudolph, they concluded that their relationship was based mainly on lust and not love. They talked more about one another's physical features and what they could do with and for one another physically. As you saw, she is a beautiful young lady, and, yes, I know back then she loved the Lord. I believe she still loves the Lord, but she has allowed the devil to step in."

"Ron, can we just pray right now?" asked Mrs. Taylor.

"Yes, can we?" said Mrs. Belkin.

Mr. Taylor held out his hands, and they all prayed.

Soon after, Mason and Danielle left out of the guest bedroom, and the closer they got to the kitchen door, they could hear the prayers going up. They also joined in.

Once the prayer was over, Mrs. Belkin asked them, "Are you two alright?"

Mason and Danielle looked at each other, and Mason answered, "We will be, and I want to apologize to all of you for all that has happened this morning. I know that Danielle is my wife, and I will not allow the devil to come in to hinder or take anything."

Danielle said, "Can we eat breakfast now? My stomach is starting to say things I do not like."

They all laughed a little, and her mother said, "Yes, but it will be a few minutes because some things need to be warmed up."

"That's fine. Mason, do you want some coffee?" Danielle asked.

"Yes, dear that would be great." Mason went and sat at the table.

Everyone else was at the table already.

Danielle brought the coffee over and sat down. When she was seated, she leaned over to him and asked, "Mason remember in our counseling session about a month ago you told Pastor Rudolph and me about you and Eboni's past relationship? Was what just happened this morning what you were asking us to pray concerning?"

"Yes, exactly," he answered.

Breakfast was over, and it was very good.

"I am totally full. There is no more room in the inn," Mr. Taylor said as everyone chuckled.

Mason looked at Danielle and said, "Danielle, do you like this on Saturday mornings?"

She looked at him. "Maybe on some Saturday mornings if our schedules allow it." She then said, "Let me get this kitchen cleaned up so I can get moving."

"I will help. You know we both have a big day today," Mason said. "You two go for a walk, and we will do the kitchen. Right, guys?" Temperance said as she looked at everyone else at the table."

"Yes, of course," they all responded together.

Danielle looked at Mason and said, "Yes, I think we need to walk and talk about our day tomorrow.

Mason answered, "Yes, we can. I will get the jackets."

They left out of the kitchen. Mason helped Danielle put her jacket on, and they walked out the front door.

"I believe they are going to be alright. We know that there is a test before every marriage. Elaine and I went through a time where she actually called off the wedding two days before we were going to get married," said Mr. Belkin.

"What? What happened for her to do that?" asked Mrs. Taylor.

"Well, it was somewhat like Mason and Danielle's situation. Not one but two women came up against me. One I had broken up with when we were dating, and the other one I broke off the engagement with her. They would call Elaine's job and tell her all types of things. The straw that broke the camel's back for her was when they both called at separate times with the same story. They told her, during a day when I was sick, that I was intimate with them at my apartment," Mr. Belkin shared.

Mrs. Taylor asked, "So, what did they say that made her think what they were saying was true?"

"Well, they told her that I was intimate with them both in separate rooms. They told her how my apartment was, like where my living room was and the layout of the bathroom. The day I was sick, Dominique, the one I cut off the engagement with, brought me some soup. We talked for a little bit then she asked if she could use the restroom. I told her sure. Apparently when she went to the bathroom, she had some of her and the other young lady, Kimberly's undergarments in the purse she had. She left them in a box in my bedroom closet. They told her the colors of the undergarments and that I was pretending to be sick. So, when she got off work that evening, she came over, we talked, and then she asked me if they had been over, and I told her that Dominique brought me some soup and that Kimberly called to check on me the day before. At the time she came over, I was up walking around. Apparently, Dominique told her about the undergarments and where they were in my bedroom. She said, 'If that is true then follow me.' I followed her to my bedroom. She looked in my closet and took those undergarments right out of that box. She said, 'I cannot do this right now. There are too many lies being told.' I was trying to explain, but she threw the undergarments on my bed and said, 'If this is what you want, go for it.' Then she walked out my front door. Oh, and she placed the ring I gave her on my dresser," Mr. Belkin said.

"Wow. So, what happened after that? Or must I say, how did God move for you?" they asked.

"I tried to call and talk to her twice. I did not know anything about the undergarments, and I left her a message both times. We were to get married that Sunday after service. This happened on a

Thursday. So, what I did was, I called our pastor who was going to officiate our wedding. I told him everything that happened. He told me to begin to pray and fast and to give her a call on Saturday. I said to him, 'But pastor we are to be married on Sunday.' He said, 'Son, I know, just do what I say and trust God.' So, I did do what he said while trusting God. I called her around seven that Saturday morning. She answered the phone, and the first thing I said was Elaine please don't hang up. I told her that I did not know how the undergarments got in that box in my closet and that I had not been with anyone. She listened. After I finished talking, she said, 'Ralph, I believe you. Yesterday I talked to Dominique and Kimberly. See the Lord showed me that they were not being truthful. Who gets intimate with two women, cleans their undergarments, and neatly places them in an empty box? I asked them both why did they lie on you, and why they do not want to see you happy. I told them that they have to move on because you and I will get married Sunday.' She said she guessed they saw that she was not budging. They apologized, and we did get married that Sunday."

Mrs. Belkin said, "Ralph, you left a lot of things out of that story; however, it did happen, and I am glad we both prayed and fasted during that time. I believe we need to do that with Mason and Danielle for a few days. What do you think?"

They all agreed to pray and fast for and with them.

Temperance, Joi', Syncere, Sonya, Cicely, Quintin, Jason, Craig, and Dillan came out of the kitchen, making fun of one another.

Mrs. Taylor asked, "What do you guys think about praying and fasting with us for a few days for Mason and Danielle?"

They said yes.

Mrs. Belkin explained that it would only be on Thursdays and Fridays up until the week they got married, which was two months away. Fasting would be Thursday and Friday until six in the evening.

Mason and Danielle got back from their walk and hung up their jackets. They then informed everyone to join them in a fast.

Temperance said, "Danielle's mom just asked us about the same thing."

"Wow, we are already beginning to think like mother and daughter," said Danielle.

Meanwhile, Eboni was on her way back home. She called her brother. "What's going on, Sis?"

"Hey big baby, guess what?"

"You won the lottery," he said chuckling.

She said, "No. I believe the Lord is answering my prayers."

"What prayer is that?" he asked.

"The one about me getting Mason back, of course. I just left the young woman Danielle's house, and I was almost able to give Mason a kiss until he pushed me away. She's not even all that cute anyway."

"What?" he yelled. "Eboni, I need you at my house as soon as you get on this side of town."

She showed up fifteen minutes later.

"Eboni, what is your problem?" asked Alex.

"I do not have a problem. Mason does. He knows I am to be his wife," she said.

"Okay, I tell you what, Eboni, let's fast for the next month, every Wednesday, Thursday, and Friday until six in the evening. If this is to be changed, you and I know that only God can make that change," said Alex.

"I will do that Alex," said Eboni.

CHAPTER 10:
No Weapon Formed Shall Prosper II

"Well, gentlemen, I guess we need to go and run the errands we need to run before the parties in a few hours?" said Mr. Taylor. The men left out the door.

"Well, ladies, what about we go to the mall for a little while? I have some coupons for some different stores in the mall," said Mrs. Taylor.

"Let's meet back here in the living room in five minutes," said Mrs. Belkin.

Mason was the designated driver for the day. He told his dad and soon to be father-in-law that he needed to get a wedding band to go to Danielle's ring. "Can we stop by some stores so I can look at some bands to get the right one that I believe fits her and the ring?"

"Sure, let's go," said Mr. Taylor and Mr. Belkin.

So, they drove a few miles and came to Jared's. They looked at some bands there, but Mason did not see anything that caused a spark. They searched for about forty-five minutes. Mason still did not see anything that he liked, so they left to go to another store.

Mason thought for a moment and said, "Dad and Mr. Belkin, I did see a few bands that I really liked at KAYS. Let's go there."

"Okay. Let's go," they said.

So, they drove a few more miles to KAYS. When Mason walked in, he went straight to the rings section. There were several that he saw and liked, but there was this one ring with a band that kept sticking out to him every time he walked by it. It was a one carrot marquis cut diamond, on a gold band and a single gold band with it. The price was also within his budget. He really liked it and knew that Danielle would really like it.

He showed it to his dad, and the rest of the crew. They all thought it was Danielle all the way.

Mason spoke to the salesperson, and they made the transaction.

They left the store, and Mason was smiling from ear to ear. Everyone was happy.

As they were getting into Mason's vehicle, he received a phone call from his sister, Temperance.

"Mason, I am calling you because Danielle, her mom, and her sisters have been in a bad car accident. I have already called 911, and the dispatcher said the first responders should be here shortly."

"Where are you guys?" Mason asked in a panic.

"We are at the intersection of Third and Rodchester."

"We will be right there," Mason said. He hung up the phone and told the men what happened, and they prayed as they headed to the scene.

"Are they okay?" everyone asked.

"Temperance did not say. We just need to get there quickly."

Back at the scene of the accident, the first responders were there. "Ma'am, can you hear me?" The fireman asked Danielle, but she is unresponsive at the moment. He knocked on the window and asked again.

She slowly looked over at him and nodded her head, yes. She was moaning and seemed to be in a lot of pain.

Her mother was sitting in the passenger seat in somewhat of a daze because of the impact of the hit. She had a deep cut on her forehead that was bleeding pretty badly.

The fireman asked his partner to check on the young lady in the seat behind Danielle, which was her sister Cicely, who was also badly hurt. Danielle's side got hit the hardest. The red Ford F-150 pickup that hit them slammed into the driver's side. Cicely had blood coming down her forehead, and she was unable to feel her left leg. Her left arm also didn't look right to the fireman.

At this time, the ambulance arrived. As the paramedics got out of the ambulance, they quickly carried a stretcher.

"Hey, we need a stretcher over here, maybe two. The driver's side of this Tahoe SUV is dented in really bad."

They actually had to cut Danielle and Cicely's doors off to get them out. The paramedics also called another ambulance for her sister, Cicely.

Minutes later, as the men drove up to the scene of the accident, Mason looked at Danielle's vehicle and started speaking in his heavenly language as he prayed. They saw Mrs. Belkin and Sonya sitting at the back of the ambulance being assisted by a paramedic. He saw Temperance, his mom, Joi', and Syncere standing by Temperance's SUV.

When Mason parked, all the guys rushed out and ran over to where Temperance's vehicle was, inquiring about what happened.

"Mason, Danielle had stopped at the stop sign. When she started going into the intersection to go across, out of nowhere the big red F-150 crashed into them," Temperance explained.

"Quintin and Jason, will you two stay here while the rest of us go see what is going on?" Mason and the other men went over to Danielle's vehicle. At this time, the other ambulance was arriving at the scene so that they could get Cicely out of the vehicle and to the hospital along with Danielle. They got Cicely out of the vehicle and onto a stretcher and took her to the other ambulance.

Mason asked Quintin and Jason to stay at the accident site until the wrecker picked up Danielle's vehicle. Once all was clear, he would let them know which hospital they took the ladies to. "Temperance, can everyone else fit in your vehicle and you follow the ambulances to the hospital?" Mason asked.

She answered yes, and Mason got into the ambulance with Danielle. Dillan was already in the ambulance with Cicely. Everyone else got into Temperance's vehicle, which had a third-row seat.

She followed the ambulance to the hospital.

Meanwhile, Eboni was at the mall with her friends. They were just walking, talking, and doing a little window shopping. "Hey, ladies, I went over to Danielle's house this morning."

"Who is Danielle?" asked Hope.

"Danielle is supposedly Mason's fiancée."

With a gasp, Hope asked, "What? Eboni, why did you do

that?"

"Girl, you know Mason is my husband, and I do not understand why he is playing with Danielle's feelings. I even almost kissed him until he pushed me away. As I told my brother, Alex, she might be cute and all, but she cannot do for him what I can," Eboni exclaimed.

Shannon chimed in. "Eboni, this is starting to get very bad. You need to move on and allow Mason to move on."

Eboni stopped and looked at Shannon. "Don't ever tell me to move on. He should have waited for me," she said, rolling her eyes.

They continued to walk, but in her peripheral view, she saw this guy watching her.

"E, do you know that guy? He has been watching you for a while."

"Girl, I don't know who he is. I noticed him watching me. You know I have a man," Eboni responded.

"Yeah, a man with a woman," Shannon said.

Eboni looked at her and rolled her eyes.

Hope and Cherish chuckled.

As they continued to walk, they looked up and saw the strange guy walking towards them. He walked up to Eboni and said, "Hi, I am Houston Livingston IV. I knew I would meet someone beautiful today."

Eboni asked, "What other tired line you got?"

"Oh, so, you want me to keep going? Because I have more tired lines, as you say, to give."

They all looked at one another and laughed.

"My name is Eboni Cutler, and I already have a man," Eboni said.

"Are you sure about that?"

They all looked at him in amazement.

"Can we walk and talk? I promise not to try anything," Said Houston.

Eboni looked at her friends.

Shannon said, "Go ahead, E. We have our eyes on you and him."

She looked back at Houston and said, "Okay, let's walk and talk."

"So why are you so hard on men or me, to be exact?" Houston asked Eboni.

"Look, five years ago I was engaged to be married to a guy. We did not get married because we believed that we were not the one for each other, but now I believe differently," Eboni replied.

"What do you believe now?" asked Houston.

"I believe I heard wrong from God. I believe he and I are supposed to be getting married in the next two months instead of him and someone else."

"So, he has moved on, and you are stuck?" he asked.

"Okay, so let's say I am stuck. How do I get unstuck?"

He answered. "Prayer, first of all, is key. Can we talk over some dinner later?"

She responded, "Sure. I will give you a chance. Where do you want to meet?"

"Meet me at Red Lobster tomorrow evening, and, yes, I am praying I will see you there." He walked away, and she went back to where her friends were.

"So, what's going on?" asked Shannon as they all looked at

her to see and hear her response.

She responded, "Okay, so, I have somewhat of a date. I am not looking for anything. I am just seeing what could happen if I think about trying to move on."

They smiled at her and gave her a hug.

Shannon said, "That's my girl."

Eboni looked at Hope and Cherish and said, "Alright, ladies, I have enjoyed the fellowship, but Shannon and I must get back to the salon."

"Yes, we do have clients in an hour," Shannon added.

They all left out the door of the mall. "I will see you ladies later on this week," Eboni said.

She got in her truck and called her brother. The phone rang twice, and he answered.

"What's up, Sis?"

"Hey, Bro. I just met a guy that I am having dinner with tomorrow evening, and I want to know if you could be there in case anything happens or goes down?"

"I got you, Sis. Where will you be and at what time?"

She responded, "We will be at the Red Lobster on Sand Dust and Roberts at seven 'o clock tomorrow evening."

He said, "Okay, I will be there."

Back at the hospital, Danielle was being prepped for surgery. Her left arm was broken, she had two cracked ribs, her left leg was broken in one place, and her left thigh bone was shattered, as shown on the body scan. That was why she needed surgery.

Cicely, on the other hand, only had a broken left arm and left leg. She also had some minor cuts and bruises on her forehead and the left side of her face from where the window broke on her side of the vehicle.

Sonya and Mrs. Belkin were okay with only a few cuts and bruises. The cut on Mrs. Belkin's forehead was not deep. It just looked bad at the time.

Everyone was in the waiting room, including Quintin and Jason, when the nurse came out to let them know what was going on. Firstly, she told them about Cicely then she explained Danielle's prognosis. She had a broken arm, two cracked ribs, her left leg was broken, and the left thigh bone was shattered. She was on her way to surgery now concerning the shattered thigh bone.

Mason asked, "How long will the surgery be?"

The nurse answered, "About four to five hours.

Craig asked, "Mason, may me and Sonya use your vehicle to go back to the hotel to check on the children and to let them know what is going on?"

"Me and Jason will ride back to the hotel with them, so we can get our vehicles. We will be praying man," Quintin said. They gave everyone a hug before leaving.

Since they had a long wait, Mason went to the chapel to pray. He said, "Lord, show me what all of this means. Help me to understand what is going on. Help me, Lord. He then got quiet. Even though his mouth was quiet, he was still battling within his spirit. While he was quiet, he heard a voice say, "Do you trust Me?"

He looked around and saw no one in the chapel with him. He then looked up and said, "Lord, yes, I trust You. I can do nothing without You." After realizing it was the Spirit of the Lord, he continued to kneel in quietness.

After a while, he stood up and thanked God for all things. Then he went back to the waiting room to check on the rest of the family.

Meanwhile, back at the salon, Shannon was watching the afternoon news report. "Eboni, did you say something about

Mason working with a girl named Danielle?"

"Yes. Why do you ask?" Eboni asked.

"If this is her, then it looks like she was in a really bad accident."

Eboni walked around the corner and said, "That is her, and did they say anything about my Mason?"

"No, they just say she is lucky to have no life-threatening injuries."

"Well, that's good. I'm just concerned about my Mason," Eboni said.

Shannon looked at Eboni, shook her head, and went to check on her client who was under the hair dryer.

Danielle had been in surgery for three and a half hours.

Nurse Salters came out to talk to the family. She said, "Ms. Danielle is a trooper. She did sustain some bad injuries, but they are not life-threatening. However, she does have a road to recovery ahead of her. She will not be able to put any pressure on that left leg at all for the next two weeks. Right now, she is in her recovery room. When she wakes up, I will come and let you guys know."

Meanwhile, Dillan and Cicely's two daughters were in Cicely's room with her. "Babe, do you need anything? I'm going to get me and the girls something to eat and to check on things concerning Danielle," Dillan said while putting on his jacket and picking up his keys.

The girls said, "Ssh, Dad, Mom is sleeping."

He then whispered, "Okay, girls, what do you two want to eat?"

The oldest daughter, Sherelle, whispered, "Dad, see what everyone else is eating and maybe we can eat with them while Mom is asleep."

"I will check." He left out the room door to check on everyone in the waiting room.

When he went into the waiting room, he saw everyone was happy and Mason was talking to a nurse. When Mr. and Mrs. Belkin saw him, they asked how Cicely was doing. "She is good. Now she is sleeping."

"How are you, Mama Belkin? You know Cicely is going to have a fit when she sees you with these stitches, cuts, and bruises," Said Dillan.

She responded, "I am good. Trust me, it looks way worse than it feels."

Mason was done talking to the nurse and wanted to know how Cicely was doing. Dillan was also curious about how Danielle was doing. "She will be fine, even though she has a road to full recovery ahead of her. She is in recovery now, and they will let us know when she wakes up," said Mason.

"Hey Dillan, Sonya, and I will go and get food. You stay with Cicely and the girls," said Craig. Then Craig asked, "Is there any particular food everyone wants to eat?"

"Chicken never fails. Chicken with sides and something to drink," said Mrs. Taylor.

Sonya said, "Let's go to Ollie's Chicken and More."

So, Sonya and Craig left to go get the food. On their way to get the food, Craig said to Sonya, "Babe, it has been a while, but these streets still look pretty much the same."

Craig used to travel through Manchester for business. He did a lot of consultation for different businesses. He would come to Manchester for business meetings.

At the chicken spot, Craig parked, got out, and went to open the door for his wife, Sonya. He asked, "Babe, are you sure you feel okay to go in here?"

"Honey, I am good. A few scrapes and that is all."

They went and were welcomed by the staff.

"Wow, their food must be good. This line is a little long," Said Sonya.

"Babe, when you taste it, you might want to take some home."

They waited in line for a few minutes. When they get to the register, the owner was there, and he said, "Craig Staples, is that you?"

"Hey, Manford, how are you?" Craig asked.

"Man. I am good, and as you see, business is steady going. How are you?" Manford asked.

"I am good. This is my wife, Sonya. Her, her mom, and her sisters were in that accident today at Third and Rodchester, and she only sustained some scrapes."

"Wow, I'm sorry to hear that. How are your mom and sisters, ma'am?" Manford inquired.

"They are well. My sister, Danielle, has a road to recovery ahead of her, but she will be fine."

"Well, what do you and the family need? Whatever it is, it is on me. I pray every one of your family members that was injured will recover speedily in Jesus' name," said Manford.

"Thanks, man," Craig said.

"Yes, thank you," Sonya said.

At the salon, Shannon and Eboni were getting hungry. "I have a taste for chicken," said Shannon.

"Well, here is fifteen dollars. Get me a three-piece mixed with mashed potatoes and broccoli florets for my sides. Also, a large, sweet tea for my drink," Eboni said.

"Alright, I will be back in a little bit," Shannon said.

In a short while, Shannon returned with the food. "Eboni, is Danielle's family rich?"

"I don't know. Why do you ask?" Eboni responded.

"Well, her sister and her sister's husband were in front of me at Ollie's Chicken and More. Even though her sister had a few scratches, she was snatched and dressed."

"Did you see Mason?" asked Eboni.

"Eboni! I said Danielle's sister and her sister's husband. I believe they were getting food for the family to take back to the hospital," Shannon angrily explained.

Hours later, the salon was about to be closed. "E, are you almost finished?" Shannon asked.

"Give me a moment to dry out this sink then we can go."

They turned off the lights as they left out the door. Eboni looked at Shannon and said, "Shannon, do you want to go get something to eat and just talk for a moment? I need some time to be in a calm mode before I get home."

Shannon responded, "E, just so you know, what you just said sounds weird. Most people go home, run some nice warm to hot temperature bath water, put on some music and while they are in the bathtub, they have a glass of wine. Okay, you can skip the glass of wine, but you get what I'm saying."

"Yes, Shannon, I get what you are saying. I just need to talk and for you to just listen," Eboni said.

"E, I got you. Where do you want to go?" Shannon asked.

"Let's go to Fredrick's Bar," Eboni said.

"Oh, we gonna be fancy. Huh?" said Shannon.

"Shannon, just come on. We can take my car. I will drop you

off to get your car later," Eboni responded.

They left to go out and eat.

Now on their way back to the hospital, Craig and Sonya were talking. "Babe, we are going to take this food to the hospital and collect our food to go. I want to get you back to the hotel so you can get some rest," Craig said.

"Okay, honey, but I feel okay."

"I know, babe, and I also know that you are going to feel the blow of the accident more tomorrow," Craig explained.

They made it back to the hospital. He dropped Sonya off at the entrance to the hospital doors. He then went to park.

Craig let everyone know he was taking his family back to the hotel so Sonya could get a nice hot bath in some Epsom salt and rest. They hugged the family. Craig, Sonya, and their girls left the hospital.

Back in the waiting area, Mason had left to visit Danielle's room. He wanted some time with her before the others came to the room to see her.

Mason walked into the recovery room where Danielle was. She was awake. When he walked in, he saw that she looked sad and that she had been crying. He approached the side of her bed and asked, "Danielle, baby, what's wrong?"

She looked at him and answered with a feeling of frustration, "Mason, look at me. It's not supposed to be like this. We should be getting married in a couple of months, Mason. What did I do? Where is God right now?"

"Danielle, baby, you are here. You are alive, and you are going to be whole. Yes, it is going to take a while, but you are going to be whole. I am going to marry you no matter how you come down the aisle. God showed me that you are my wife several times. Danielle, what does Romans chapter eight verse twenty-eight say?" Mason asked.

She muttered, "All things work together for good to those that love God and are called to His purpose. Okay, Mason, what good can come out of this?"

"Danielle, can we pray?"

"Yes, please, Mason, because I do not understand what God is up to right now."

Mason gently held her hand and began to pray.

CHAPTER 11:
The Next Day

The next morning, Danielle woke up to the sound of someone in the restroom. In astonishment, she looked and waited to see who it was. When the restroom door opened, out came Mason. "Mason, did you stay overnight?" she asked.

"Danielle, I did not mean to wake you, and, yes, I did stay overnight. I believe that this is a part of God's plan for us at this very moment. Last night, I got a chance to spend some valuable time with you," Mason said.

"Mason, you really do not have to do any of this. I don't want you to miss out on the things you have planned for later because of me," Danielle exclaimed.

"I am not missing out on anything. I am on my way to today's service. I will be back after service, and we can talk more about this," he said as he leaned in and kissed her on her forehead.

On the way to church, Mason thought about Danielle and prayed for her concerning the conversation they had before he left the hospital.

When he got to the church, Quintin and Jason were just getting there. He parked his vehicle and got out. "Good morning, guys.

What's good?"

"We are good, man. How are you, and how is Danielle?" asked Jason.

"I am good, but Danielle is having somewhat of a hard time because of the accident. Can we talk after service?"

"Sure, Mason," said Jason. They hugged, and all three walked into the church together.

Church services were amazing. The Spirit of the Lord was all over the place. After service, Mason stood alongside his parents shaking hands and hugging other members of the church.

Once the members were out of the church and Mason made sure all the lights were off and the doors were locked, he told his parents that he was going back to the hospital to check on Danielle and he would call them later.

Outside, he saw Quintin and Jason waiting on him. "Oh, yeah, I almost forgot about Quintin and Jason. I will call you later, Mom and Dad," said Mason.

"Okay, Son, and see you later, boys," Said Mr. and Mrs. Taylor.

Jason and Quintin said their goodbye to Mason's parents.

Mason then walked over.

"What's up, Mason? What did you want to talk to us about?" asked Quintin.

"Well, Danielle is having a hard time accepting all that the accident is dishing out to her. Like, last night she was saying that things were not supposed to be like this and where is God in this situation? I prayed with her. This morning, she woke up while I was in the restroom, and when I came out, she asked me if I stayed the night with her at the hospital. You two know me. Why should her parents have to be at the hospital with her all night when she is going to become my wife? I just wanted to take care of what I believe God is giving to me," Mason said.

"Mason, I understand you, but I want you to try to understand her perspective. Communicate with her about how you are. Express to her exactly what you are telling us now. She needs to feel God's love from you because apparently something happened before God placed you in her life," Jason explained.

"Well, I am getting ready to go to the hospital now to see if she is hungry and get her what she needs," said Mason.

"Alright, let's pray before we depart," Jason said, and he led them in prayer.

After the prayer, they hugged each other and went their

separate ways.

Mason got back to the hospital and went to Danielle's room. When he got to her room door, he overheard her talking to the nurse, so he just stood and listened.

"Whoever the guy is that slept on this couch last night must really love you," said the nurse.

"Huh?" said Danielle, bewildered.

"Ma'am, while you slept last night, he made sure you were comfortable as you needed to be. Earlier this morning, I didn't know if you groaned in pain or what, but he wanted to make sure that your pain was minimal. Also, the other nurse said that he spent a lot of time in the chapel last night, and he said that he was praying for you, his future wife," the nurse explained.

"Wow," said Danielle.

After hearing enough, Mason knocked on the door.

"Come in," said Danielle.

Mason walked in and kissed Danielle on the forehead.

"Hi, Mason honey. This is Nurse Sanders," Said Danielle.

"Is everything okay?" Mason asked.

"She is doing well. She might just get a chance to go home tomorrow," Nurse Sanders said.

"That sounds great. God is so good," Replied Mason.

"Well, you are good, and I will see you in a few hours," Said Nurse Sanders. She left out the door.

"Mason, you know you don't have to do the things that you are doing," Danielle said.

"Danielle, what are you talking about?" Mason asked.

"You were here last night, and you are here now when I know you normally have other things that you do after church service."

Mason looked at her and said, "Danielle, what is it? Why do you not want me here with you? If we were married right now, where do you think I would be? I am not understanding you right now."

Danielle responded, "Mason, up until now, I have been conditioned to doing things mainly on my own. Two years ago, as I told you in one of our counseling sessions, I too was engaged to be married. He used to do some of the same things that you are doing for me now. The month before we got married, he wanted to take the intimacy to another level. He said he wanted to practice kissing me so it would not seem awkward on our wedding day. I

123

asked him why would that be awkward? That's when he dropped the bombshell about his ex-wife. He gave me no indication he was previously married. At that point, he became a lie and a liar in my eyes. That day I left his apartment without a ring on my finger."

"Danielle, I do not have an ex-wife. I have never been married before, and you have already met my ex-fiancée' which I would rather you had not met her the way you did. I truly want to be with you for the rest of my life. The only thing I can say is that you have to trust the God in me," Mason lamented. "Are you hungry?" he then asked.

She looked at him while yawning and said, "I am actually sleepy."

He took off his suit jacket and his tie and sat down and started surfing through the television channels to see what was on.

Immediately, there was a knock at the door.

Mason went and saw that it was his dad and Mr. Belkin. He whispered, "Hi Dad and Papa Belkin. She just fell asleep."

"Did you two eat anything yet?" Her father asked.

"No, sir, she said she was not hungry at the time, and neither was I. Maybe when she wakes up, I can check and see if she wants me to order something for her," Mason said.

"Son, I brought the clothes you asked for."

"Thanks, Dad." Turning to both his fathers, he said, "Dad and Mr. Belkin, Danielle still has some issue concerning her engagement break-up from two years ago. I tried to assure her that I am not like that young man and that we are two different people. I know that I cannot change that, but I know God can. I told her that she would have to trust the God in me."

Then her dad shared, "Son, her mother was the same way. Unfortunately, you have to build her trust. You both have to trust the process."

They continued to talk for a couple of hours.

Danielle woke up to them laughing and talking. "So, this is what goes on when I am getting my beauty rest?" she giggled.

They laughed, and her dad responded, "Sweetheart, it is so good to see you awake. Are you hungry, and how do you feel?"

"I am hungry, and I am a little achy, but I am alright," She answered.

"What do you want to eat?" Mason inquired.

"I have a taste for some soul food. Some collard greens, yams, cornbread, and fried chicken," Answered Danielle.

"I know just the place to order from. Dad and Papa Belkin, do you want anything?"

His dad and Mr. Belkin told him what they wanted, and he stepped out of the room and placed their orders.

While he was in the hallway, Nurse Sanders went into the room to check Danielle's vitals and see if she needed any medicine for pain. "Good evening. How is my patient this evening?"

"I am a little achy and a bit hungry. My fiancé is getting me something to eat though," Danielle answered.

Nurse Sanders then asked, while checking her vitals, "Do you need anything for pain?"

"No, I do not believe I need any pain meds because I am not in that much pain. My pain level might be at level 5, if that," Danielle said.

"Your vitals look good, so I will see you in a few hours. Just pull the string if you need me," Nurse Sanders said before walking out of the room.

Just then, Mason came back and told them the orders were placed and will be ready for pick up in about ten minutes.

When the food arrived, everyone enjoyed every bit of it.

"Omg! Mason this food is so good. Where did you get it from, and do they cater?" Danielle asked.

"I got this from Shoney's Soul food downtown."

"Yes, Son, you really did it this time," said Mr. Belkin.

"Thanks, Papa Belkin. It is my pleasure, and I am glad you are enjoying it."

They ate and talked for about an hour before both their dads left.

Back at Eboni's house, she was in preparation mode for her date. "I wonder if this red dress will work for tonight?" Eboni said to herself while looking in a long length mirror with the dress in front of her. She eventually paired it with some gold accessories and red and gold heels. "Yasss! Yasss! I can do this. Let me call Alex and remind him of the semi date tonight."

She then called Alex and reminded him about her meet up at seven that evening with Houston.

Since it was fifteen minutes after five, she went to get her shower, so she could get ready for what she was calling her semi date.

About an hour and a half later, Eboni walked into the Red

Lobster. She was really feeling herself as she swayed her hips from side to side.

Houston walked up to her and said, "Come with me, ma'am." He held out his hand to her, and she placed her hand in his, and they walked to a table that he reserved for them.

As they walked to the table, she looked at him and noticed that he also had red, black, and gold colors on. She wondered, "How did he know I was going to wear these colors?"

When they got to the table, she said thank you as he pulled out her chair so she could sit down.

He said, "You are welcome, ma'am."

The waitress came over and asked, "What would you like to drink?"

Houston allowed her to say what she wanted to drink first.

"I will go get your drinks and give you time to look at the menu to see if you would like appetizers before your meal and dessert. Is that okay?" the waitress said.

"That will be fine," answered Houston.

They looked at the menu to see what they wanted to eat as far as an appetizer, entrée, and a dessert. When the waitress returned, they placed their orders but held off on dessert just in case their stomachs were too full.

"So, this thing about you being stuck. Do you care to explain it?" Houston asked. "Well, exactly five years ago, I was in a relationship with a young man whom I believe was an amazing young man then and now. We were engaged to be married. We cut off the engagement and the wedding because we believe that the Lord had us for other people. Meaning, I am to marry someone else, not him. He is to marry someone else, not me. Now I believe that we did not hear God right," she explained as the waitress brought the appetizers.

"Do you think God will tell you something and then change His mind about what He told you?" Houston asked.

"Well, no. I just believe that we heard wrong," Eboni said.

"Well, does this guy you are talking about think the same way you do?"

"What does that have to do with what I believe? What if he does not believe what I believe? What if he plans to marry another woman in a couple of months?" she asked.

"Hold up," Houston said while putting his fork down on his plate. "Did you just say he is about to marry another woman in a couple of months?"

"Yes," she said as she placed her hand on her forehead.

Houston reached over and grabbed her other hand that was still on the table. "Look at me." When she looked at him, he asked, "Have you ever thought about moving on?"

"No, because he is to be marrying me. We are to be sharing the house he stays in. Why are you asking me about this anyway?"

He answered, "Well, you said you are stuck. If you do not decide to move on and ask the Lord to heal the hurt, you will be stuck forever."

"I do not want to be stuck, but I do not want to give up on a dream either," she said.

"Is it a dream for him or for you?" he asked.

She sighed and asked, "Can we finish eating now?"

"Oh, yes. Just think about it, Eboni. You are better than this."

Then they went back to eating their meal.

Afterwards, Houston paid for their meals, and he walked Eboni to her truck.

She looked at him and said, "Houston, thank you for asking me out tonight. Thank you for talking and listening to me concerning a wound that I never allowed to be healed. I will pray about what we talked about."

"Eboni, it was my pleasure to listen to you and take the band-aid off the wound, but in all seriousness, please think and pray about the talk we had. Do you think we can meet again sometime next week?" he asked.

"Sure. I don't see why not."

"May I get your number, so I can call you?"

She looked at him and said, "I thought you would never ask. Here you go." She wrote it down on a napkin and gave it to him.

He said, "I will call you to see what day and time will be good for you."

"I look forward to your call," she said.

He opened her truck door, so she could go in. He said, "Well, I will see you next week. I am calling you now so that you can call me or text me when you get home. Let me know when you have made it home safely."

"I will," she said.

As she drove off, she called her brother.

"Are you okay, Sis?"

She said, "Yes, Bro. I am calling to let you know everything was good, and I will be meeting with him again sometime this coming week. I will not need you to come this time. I believe he is good for me right now. I will talk to you later."

"Alright, Sis. Just let me know if you need me."

"Okay, Bro. I love you."

"I love you, too, Sis."

They hung up, and her mind drifted to everything that she and Houston discussed over dinner. After thinking for a few moments, she began to pray. She said, "Lord, help me. I do not want to stay stuck."

She continued to pray all the way home.

Meanwhile, at the hospital, Mason was in the chapel while Nurse Sanders was helping Danielle with a bath. He prayed concerning their relationship. "Lord, I know I will have to build Danielle's trust in me, and I have to trust her. Please continue to order my steps to be the best fiancé and to become the husband you need me to be for her. Amen."

He looked up and saw Nurse Sanders coming towards him.

"Is everything alright, Nurse Sanders?"

"Everything is okay. You two must love each other a lot. She asked me twice if you were coming back. She is head over heels for you."

He responded, "Nurse, you have it backwards. I am head over heels for her. After God, she is the one."

"Well, Mr. Knight in Shining Armor, please go and be with your princess because she awaits your presence," said the Nurse.

"I am on my way there now," he said.

She smiled at him and went back to the nurse's station as he went back to Danielle's room.

Hours passed, and Mason fell asleep. He woke up to Danielle praying. He just laid there still praying along with her.

There was a knock at her room door. It was Nurse Stacey, the morning nurse, along with Dr. Waller. The nurse checked her vitals, and Dr. Waller went over the plans they had for the day.

"In about an hour, Nurse Devon and Nurse David will come get you to take you for a ride in a wheelchair and to help you get started on figuring out how to use crutches. After which you will be on your way home. Are you in any pain or do you need anything before we get you your breakfast?" asked Dr. Waller.

"No, sir, I am okay, just still a little achy. My pain level is probably level five right now. If I start hurting more than what I am at now, I will pull the string and let Nurse Stacey know." Danielle answered.

"Alright, young lady. I will see you in a few hours," Dr. Waller said. He and Nurse Stacey left out the room door.

Ten minutes later her breakfast arrived. She asked Mason if he wanted to try some, but he was not hungry. They talked to one another while she ate.

Nurse Devon and Nurse David came to take her to show her the best way to use crutches and to find the right height that is suitable for her.

Mason said, "I will be in the chapel when you are finished."

Danielle said, "No, babe, you have to come with me. I am going to need your help with this."

"Yes, sweetheart. I am right here."

As the nurses pushed her in the wheelchair, they tested her

comfort level. They told her she will have to come back to get the crutches after the cast is off her left arm.

As they were talking to her, Mason was praying, "Lord, I know that You are a healer. I ask right now in Your son Christ Jesus' name that You will allow the healing to begin in Danielle's bones and that she will have a speedy recovery. I thank You for answering my prayer in advance." He then went back to listening to what the nurses were saying to Danielle.

Back at Mason's house, Mr. Taylor woke up to the scent of bacon. He looked up and said, "Lord, I thank You for Sylvia. I am blessed beyond measure. I give You all the glory, honor, and praise for my beautiful wife of thirty-five years."

He got up, put on his robe, and went to the kitchen. He heard her singing before he entered the kitchen. He enjoyed her singing, so he just stood at the door for a few moments before he entered and said, "Good morning, my love."

She looked around at him and smiled. She went over to him, and they shared a morning kiss. "Are you ready for some breakfast?" she asked.

"Yes, I am," he answered.

"I wanted to cook us breakfast, especially since Mason has everything here at his house." She fixed his plate and her plate and brought them to the table. "You know, I am so glad Mason decided to go ahead and buy this house even though at the time he did not go through with the marriage. I do believe he heard from God back then because Danielle is the young lady God showed me in a dream one night about three years ago," said Mrs. Taylor.

"Were you ever going to tell me about this dream?" Mr. Taylor asked.

"Baby, I did not say anything at the time because Mason was still trying to figure things out between himself and Eboni. I did not want to cause any confusion. I knew that he heard what he believed was from the Lord. I knew Eboni was a woman of God, but I also knew she was not the woman God had for Mason."

"See, this is the reason I thank God for you every day. You complete me," he said as he leaned over and kissed her on the cheek.

"Have you talked to Mason this morning?" she asked.

"No. I will call him after we finish breakfast. I pray that Danielle is able to leave the hospital soon."

Meanwhile at the hospital, Danielle was brought back into the room after finding a good wheelchair. "Well, that is my exercise for today," Danielle said. She tried to wheel herself with her right arm since it was not in a cast. They helped her back into her bed, checked her vitals again, and asked if she was in any pain.

"Danielle, I will let you rest for a little bit. I will call Dad and Mama Belkin to let them know you will be discharged, and I will go to the chapel for a moment. Do you need anything from me before I leave for a little bit?" asked Mason.

"Just say a prayer for me while you are in the chapel," she said.

He went over to the right side of her bed, gently held her hand, and said, "Sweetie, I am going in the chapel to pray for us."

A few hours later, Dr. Waller came back to talk to her and Mason just to let them know he wanted to keep her in the hospital another night for observation.

The next day, the doctor returned. "How are you, young lady?" asked Dr. Waller.

"My pain level is down, thank the Lord."

"Did you sleep alright last night, sir, because I know that this bed/sofa can be a doozey?" he asked Mason.

"I slept well, sir."

"That is good. Well, I have some good news. You will be able to go home in an hour or two. Your vitals are good, and you are looking good."

Mason looked at her and just smiled.

"Well, I have to finish making my rounds with my other patients. I will have Nurse Salters come in and walk you through the meds that I have prescribed for you. Do you need anything before I leave?" said Dr. Waller.

"Do you need anything, honey?" Mason asked.

"No, I don't need anything right now," Danielle answered.

"Alright, Nurse Salters will be in here in a little while."

Ten minutes after Dr. Waller left, Mr. Taylor called Mason. "Good morning, Son. I am calling to let you know that we will be there shortly and to see if you needed us to bring anything to you?"

"Good morning, Dad. We would be happy to see you and Mom. We have some great news to tell you. Did Mom cook this morning, and if she did, is there anything left?"

"Yes, she did cook, and we do have some breakfast left. I will make sure we warm it up and get it packed for you two. We will be there shortly."

Later on, there was a knock, on Danielle's hospital room door. It was Mason's dad and mom along with Danielle's dad and mom.

"Hi, family. She just fell asleep," he whispered.

"Look at her, Ralph. She sleeps so peacefully," said Mrs. Belkin. "She sleeps just like you, dear."

They looked at each other and smiled.

"So, Son, what is the good news you have to share with us?"

"First of all, Mom Belkin, are you doing okay?"

"I am sore, but I had to come check on Danielle," she said.

"Well, I wanted Danielle to be awake so that she could tell you the good news," Mason said.

They heard Danielle stirring in her bed, and then her eyes popped open as she stared back at them. "Hi, guys, what's going on?"

"Honey, nothing is going on. Mason said you have some good news to tell us," said Mrs. Belkin.

"Yes, I wanted you to tell them the good news," Mason said.

Danielle looked at him and smiled. Then she looked at their

parents and said, "Well, the good news is I will be getting discharged in an hour or so."

Their parents were so elated for Danielle to be getting out of the hospital. "That is so great. I knew the Lord would answer our prayers. I am so grateful and thankful," said Mrs. Taylor.

Mrs. Belkin was so overjoyed she was in tears.

"Mom, why are you crying?"

"I am so happy for you, and as Sylvia said, the Lord surely answered our prayers," she answered.

"Oh, Mom. Come give your girl a hug," said Danielle.

They began to talk to one another and ate the breakfast that was brought by the Taylors.

Back at Eboni's house, she woke up prayerful and thanked God for another day. After saying her morning prayer, she went to the kitchen to get a cup of coffee. She drank it on the patio outside her bedroom as she read her devotional for the day.

After reading her devotional, she thought about all she had going on for the day. She was happy that she did not have to be at the salon until noon. She sat outside looking around at the nice view she had. She thought to herself, "It would be great to have

Mason sitting here beside me."

As she thought about that, Houston immediately came to mind. She started to think about the things they talked about last evening. She said, while sitting at the table on her patio, "Lord, why do I still believe Mason belongs with me when he is actually with another woman? I still love him, Lord. Help me, Lord. If he is not for me then send someone else to find me." She continued to talk to the Lord on her patio before getting ready for work.

When she got to the salon, Eboni talked to Mrs. Lane as she washed her hair. "So, Mrs. Lane, what did Mr. Lane say after he saw that you burnt the toast?"

Mrs. Lane answered, "He said, 'Dee, are you alright in there?' I told him, 'Yes, I just have a lot on my mind right now.' So, he came into the kitchen and said, 'Honey, some things you have to allow God to handle. Just give it to Him and leave it with Him.'"

"Wow, he is so deep. I see why you love him so much," Eboni said.

"Yes, he keeps me in the love of God, so to say," said Mrs. Lane.

"Why do you say it like that?"

Mrs. Lane answered, "I say it like that because he does what the Bible says and that is, he washes me with the word of God.”

“Really? Where is that in the Bible?” Eboni asked.

“Read the whole chapter of Ephesians five. It will help you in a lot of areas as far as marriage is concerned. Trust me, when you read that chapter, you will be glad you did.”

“I will. I really appreciate you talking with me and giving me pointers on marriage. Maybe one day soon my man will recognize he is to be with me instead of someone else,” said Eboni.

“Well, baby, I thank you for appreciating me. I give all glory to God, and about this man, sometimes we have to allow God to do what needs to be done in a situation and just trust Him in the process,” Mrs. Lane said.

She finished shampooing Mrs. Lane’s hair and began massaging in the conditioner. “I do trust him, and this process is hard. I don’t want to be doing anything on my own. I want God to be glorified in whatever I say and do but this part of the process is overwhelming.”

“I know, hun. When you trust God for things, as my husband says, when we give God something, we have to leave it with Him and trust Him in the process,” said Mrs. Lane.

“Yes, ma’am, I will put that into practice.” She finished Mrs.

Lane's hair and started on another client's hair.

Back at the hospital, one hour later, there was a knock-on Danielle's hospital room door. Mason went to open the door and in walked Nurse Salters.

"Alright, young lady, it is time for you to be released. I have the paperwork that tells you about each of the prescriptions and how to take them. I also have your discharge papers here for you to sign," Nurse Salters said. She showed her what pages to sign and where to sign them.

"Alright, give me a moment to put this paperwork in the system, get your copy, and help you into your wheelchair." She went to the nurse's station to do what she needed to do.

Mrs. Belkin and Mrs. Taylor helped Danielle to the bathroom to get dressed.

When the nurse came back, she was surprised to see Danielle in her wheelchair and Mason waiting to push her out of the room to go home.

"We are ready," Mason said.

Nurse Salters gave her the paperwork and wished her a speedy recovery. "I have greatly enjoyed being your nurse for the past few days. Don't forget your appointment in a couple of weeks," she said.

"I have enjoyed being your patient, and maybe I will see you during my appointment," said Danielle. They hugged before Danielle left.

Mason pushed Danielle out the room door. Behind him was the rest of the family, carrying all their personal items.

Once they got downstairs to the entrance doors, they helped Danielle into the vehicle, and Mason and his parents followed Danielle and her parents to her house.

Now at the house, Mason and his parents sat and talked to Danielle and her parents for a little while, until they noticed Danielle getting tired and uncomfortable. Mason and his parents decided it was time to head out.

Mason kissed Danielle on her forehead and told her that he loved her.

During the night, Danielle woke up and began to think about how she would get around with crutches and a wheelchair. She said, "Lord, what is going on right now in my life that I have to go through this process of having a cast on majority of my leg and my arm. From mid-thigh to mid-calf. This does not feel good at all. I am not enjoying this process."

After prayer, she just sat up in bed and watched the television until she fell asleep.

The next day after Mason left work, he came to check on Danielle. When he got to the house he was met at the door by her parents. He talked to them for a while to see how they were doing and also to ask about Cicely.

Cicely was released from the hospital two days before Danielle, and her, her husband, and children left yesterday to go home.

After Mason got his updates on everyone he asked if he could see Danielle.

"Oh, yes! We believe you will make her day," they said in unison.

Mason walked down the hallway to her room. When he got to her bedroom door, he knocked and waited for a response.

"Come in."

Mason opened the door, and when she saw him, her facial expression said it all.

"Hey, sweetheart, are you feeling alright?"

She looked at him in awe and said, "I am good. I am just going to have to get used to the wheelchair and crutches."

"Danielle, I am right here. I am not going anywhere. We can figure some things out together. I am just glad neither one of us have stairs in our home." He chuckled. "Now, that would be bad."

She looked at him again and said, "Mason, thank you so much for being here right now and for just being in my life period."

He looked at her. "Danielle, honey, we will be husband and wife in a month, so why not start now doing what I will be doing then?"

She smiled and said, "I love you, Mason Jerome Taylor."

"I love you more, Danielle Marie Belkin soon to be Mrs. Taylor." He sat in a chair beside her bed, and they went into a deep conversation.

While Mason was in the room talking with Danielle, his parents came over and brought dinner with them. Mr. and Mrs. Belkin were happy to see them too. They invited them inside. They talked for a little before going to get Mason and Danielle.

Mason helped Danielle out of bed and into her wheelchair. He pushed her into the living room where her mom sat on the couch.

While Danielle was in dialogue with her mom, Mason left to go help his dad and Mr. Belkin fix the plates for dinner.

Danielle sat and gleaned from the ladies. "Oh, the wisdom they have to give!" she thought to herself. As she talked with them, she said, "I love Mason. I enjoy being around him. I just cannot get around the fact of him helping to take care of me during this time with this cast on." She rolled her eyes at the cast.

"Sweetheart, everything is going to be alright. Mason loves you, and he really wants to take care of you. Do not push him away. He is the best thing for you right now," her mother said with a smile.

Mrs. Taylor smiled also and said, "Yes, I agree with your mother, and I believe that you are the best thing for him right now. See, even right now, you two are going through things together. This is how marriage works. You go through the good, the bad, and the ugly. You have to stick to it, and you have to be there for one another. Right now, it is just a test of time for you two, but I know that you both have this. You two have studied hard for this test, so just go ahead, and ace it."

Danielle looked at Mrs. Taylor with tears in her eyes and just smiled.

Mason came in from the kitchen to let them know the food

was ready and their plates were fixed.

He proceeded to push Danielle into the dining room. When he went over to get behind her wheelchair, he realized that she was teary eyed. He bent down to her ear and asked, "Sweetheart, are you okay? Have you been crying?"

"Yes, I have been crying. It has been all for a good reason, and I am learning to be content about this cast, which, right now, is very hard for me."

He kissed her forehead and pushed her to her dining room area where their parents were. He sat in his chair right beside her as Mr. Belkin prayed over the food.

They ate and had great conversations.

The week went by so quickly, and everyday Mason visited Danielle. He took work to her that she was able to complete from home, and he helped her get it done. It had been a productive week for Mason, and now the weekend was here.

Meanwhile, Eboni was on her way home from her salon. She was very tired and thinking about all the things Mrs. Lane told her as she was shampooing, conditioning, and styling her hair the other day. She also thought about her and Houston's conversation at Red Lobster. Since he was on her mind, she made a call to him.

"Good evening, Eboni. How are you today?"

"Houston, I am tired. I had a lot of clients today. One client made me think of you, so I am calling to see if we can meet at the Salt Grass restaurant one day this week. If yes, what day is best for you?"

"My answer is yes. We can meet at Salt Grass restaurant. It would have to be in the evening because I don't get off work until five o'clock every evening. The only evening, I will not be available is Wednesday because I do a Bible study at the church where my dad pastors."

She asked, "Will Thursday at seven o'clock be good for you?"

"As far as I know I have nothing planned for Thursday. I believe that will be a great evening to get together."

"Alright, I will see you then," she said.

After hanging up, she continued her drive home.

After Houston ended the call, he said a little prayer. "Lord, if Eboni is the woman You have for me then You make things happen. I do not want to be the one trying to make something happen and it is not in Your will. God, You do it. Amen"

Eboni was up getting dressed for Sunday service. She was a

member of Calvary Baptist Church. As she got dressed, she sang praises unto God and thought about her conversations with Houston and Mrs. Lane. She prayed and asked the Lord to move in the service and to have His divine way.

She left the house and headed to the house of the Lord. Eboni was ready to get what the Lord had for her from this message about love. The sermon came from First Corinthians, the thirteenth chapter. She was engaged and focused and was also thinking about how she could incorporate what she was learning from this message into the conversation she would have with Houston when they met at the restaurant.

CHAPTER 12:
There Is No Place Like Home

At Promise Keepers Ministries, the service was ending, and Mr. Belkin was doing the altar call. Mason went up front because he was one of the several ministers that prayed with those who come to the altar during this time.

After the altar call time, Mr. Taylor came up to the podium and asked Pastor Belkin to come back up to the podium also. He prayed for him and asked his members to give whatever the Lord lay on their heart to give to Mr. Belkin because he is good ground. After the offering was made for Mr. Belkin, Mr. Taylor said the benediction and ended the service.

Danielle did not attend church with everyone else, but she watched through livestream. She did not like the fact that she could not be there to hear her father minister in person. Yes, she enjoyed watching him on the livestream, but it wasn't the same as in person.

After she turned her television off, she thought about how good God has been to her and how fortunate she was to have her parents, Mason, his family, and all her friends who have supported her in this low time. She began to open her mouth and lift her voice in praise to God. She was worshipping to the point of her weeping because she was so thankful to God for what He was doing in and through her in this season of her life.

Ten minutes later, Danielle heard her parents come in, and she heard other voices too. She was trying to get herself together, but Mason knocked on her bedroom door before she could.

"Come in."

He walked in, looked at her, and said, "Sweetheart, what's wrong? Why are your eyes teary?"

"Mason, nothing is wrong. I am just so thankful right now for the people who I know truly love me and those who have been here with me through it all."

"Okay. You know I am here no matter what," he said.

"I know," she said as she wiped her cheeks. "I was just praising and worshipping God for all that He is doing in my life during this season."

"Okay, as long as you are not in pain or anything."

Right after, they began to talk about the message her dad ministered at church.

"Danielle, do you want to go outside for a little while?"

"Yes, I would love to."

He helped her get into the wheelchair. She was already dressed, so he pushed her down the hallway to the living room where her parents were sitting on the couch talking. "Dad and Mom, we are going to go outside for a little while," said Danielle.

"Alright," said Mr. Belkin as he got up to open the door.

Mason pushed her out the door to her porch. He closed the door behind them. "Do you want to stay on the porch or would you rather to be pushed around the yard for a while as we talk?"

Danielle answered, "Let's go out into the yard and talk as you push me around because I have not been out in my yard since the accident."

So, he pushed her off the porch and into her yard, and they admired the flowers.

While they were looking at the flowers, they saw Mason's parents drive up.

When they got out of the vehicle, they came with groceries stacked in their hands.

Mason and Danielle waved at them and kept talking. They talked for about forty-five minutes to an hour then he pushed her back inside. As he pushed her into the foyer of her house, he said, "I am anticipating the day I carry you through the front door of our home after we become husband and wife."

She smiled and answered, "Me too."

Mason pushed her to her living room. "Danielle, do you want to stay in here with everyone, or do you want to go back in your room to bed?" Mason asked.

"I want to stay in here with everyone. Will you help me sit in the recliner?"

"Sure, sweetheart," answered Mason.

He helped her then Mr. Belkin said, "Okay, guys, let's fix some lunch." They fixed grilled ham and cheese sandwiches with salt and black pepper kettle chips on the side. Mason made some lemonade using freshly squeezed lemons. When lunch was ready, the men opened the kitchen door to three sleeping beauties: Mrs. Belkin on the couch, Mrs. Taylor on the love seat, and Danielle in her recliner.

Mr. Taylor quietly went back into the kitchen and told Mason and Mr. Belkin the women were asleep. The men fixed plates for themselves and placed the rest of the food in containers until the women decided to wake up.

Two hours later, the ladies woke up to the sound of laughter coming from the kitchen. Mrs. Belkin and Mrs. Taylor got up and walked to the kitchen door quietly to see what the commotion was about. They could hear their husbands talking and trying to laugh quietly. They pushed the door open and walked in.

"I see two of the sleeping beauties are awake," said Mr. Taylor.

"What time is it?"

"Baby, it is three-thirty. Why?"

She looked at Mrs. Belkin and said, "Elaine, thank you so much for your hospitality because that nap was amazing."

Mrs. Belkin said, "Sylvia, anytime you want to come over for a good nap while I am here let me know."

"Are you two ready to eat?" asked Mr. Belkin.

Both ladies looked at each other then they looked at their husbands and nodded in affirmation.

"I will go check on Danielle," said Mason. He went into the living room and looked at her, and she said hi. "Hi, Danielle, are you ready for something to eat?"

"Yes, I am hungry."

"Alright, I will be right back with your plate." Mason went over to the counter and started fixing Danielle's plate. "Danielle is awake, and she is hungry. So, I am fixing her plate," he said to the others before taking the food to the living room.

"Mason, thank you so much. I just want the Lord to show me what I am to learn from this. We get married in a month, and I will still be on crutches."

"Danielle, I do not care if you hop down the aisle with one leg, even if you are in a wheelchair. I will get a chance to spend my life with you. I will pray with you about what the Lord wants to show you through this. Now eat your food, please," he said.

She looked at him, smiled, and started eating her grilled sandwich.

He sat with her for a little while, talking to her while she ate her lunch. While they were talking, Mrs. Belkin and Mrs. Taylor came into the living room because the men did not want them touching any dishes. They said they will clean the kitchen.

Two hours later, Mason and his parents got ready to leave. Mason asked Danielle, "Is there anything you need me to do before I leave? I will be back when I leave work tomorrow."

"No. I will be alright. My parents are here. They can help me out with anything I need later. They will be here to help me for the next week until my appointment. Thank you again for being here and assisting me. I really do appreciate you."

"Danielle, I am just preparing for when we get married. I love you, sweetheart," Mason said.

When Mason got home, he turned his television on in his living room to see if any games were on because it was still early in the evening.

His dad said, "Son, I am going to get changed into some more comfortable clothes." His dad went to the bedroom where they were staying for the night while his mother went to get some lemonade.

She brought Mason a glass also. "Here, Son. I believe you need a drink. Mason, you really love Danielle, huh?"

"Yes, Mom. I love her a lot. I know that she is the one God has for me."

"Son, I just needed to hear you say that, and I have had dreams concerning you and Danielle. Fairytale-like dreams. I am so happy the Lord brought her into your life," she said. She sipped on her lemonade and sat watching some of the game with him.

His dad came back to the living room and sat.

"Son, I will see you in the morning. Babe, I will see you in a little bit," his mom said.

Mason and his dad finished watching the game.

When the game was over, Mason turned the volume on the tv down, and they started to chat. "Dad, I am thinking about talking to Danielle about moving the wedding date back. What do you think?"

His dad responded, "Son, was there a reason you want to move the date back? And it is really not up to me about the date. This will be you and Danielle's day, the date you two pick."

"Well, Dad, Danielle really does not want to come down the aisle on crutches, with a wheelchair, or with a cane. I would like her to walk down the aisle with her father by her side. I want her to be the confident woman I know she is on that day."

"Son, yes, talk it over with Danielle, and whatever date you two decide on will be the date we will work with."

"Thanks, Dad. I knew you would give me some wisdom on this issue," said Mason.

"You are welcome. I am happy that you even think to talk to

me about these things." They smiled and hugged. "Now, Son, I must go to bed because you know your mother is waiting on me."

Mason stayed in the living room for a little bit until his eyes were tired. To finish out the night, he took a shower, prayed, and went to bed because he had work early in the morning.

Mason and his parents went to see Danielle and her parents all that week. This brought much unity and strength to their family.

CHAPTER 13:
Do I Trust You, Lord?

Thursday morning, Eboni woke up feeling extremely anxious. She prayed for her day and for her date with Houston. She fixed herself a cup of coffee and went out on her patio to relax while she read her daily devotional. She kept check of the time because she had a client coming in about three hours. She had a pretty full day today ahead of her. She ended her devotion, thanking God in advance for a lovely day.

She got a shower, got dressed, and headed to the salon.

At work, Eboni did not get a break because there were numerous clients coming in and out.

Once she ended her day at five that evening, she went home to get ready. She had just enough time to get in the door, shower, and head out.

When she got to the restaurant, Houston was sitting in the lobby area waiting. He saw her walking to the door. He was truly a gentleman. When he saw her approaching, he opened the door for her. "Good evening, Eboni," he said.

She looked at him as she was walking through the door and told him, "Good evening, Houston."

He turned his attention to the hostess because he had reserved a table for them in advance.

"Alright, look at you, making me feel special and all."

"Eboni, you are special," Houston said. The waiter came to the table, and they ordered their drinks. While they waited, they shared the happenings of the day with each other.

A few minutes later, the waiter brought their drinks, and they ordered their food at the same time. They then continued their conversation. "Eboni, your brown eyes are so beautiful to me. I don't mean to get off the subject, but they are," said Houston.

She looked at him, smiling shyly, and responded, "Thank you."

"You are welcome, Eboni. See, Eboni, you have to know that just because God said no about one person, He did not say no about all persons," Houston said.

"What do you mean?" Eboni asked.

"I mean, we have been to three restaurants in the past couple of weeks. I do not consider them dates because you are just now warming up to me. The first couple of times you had a big attitude, and it stunk. I know that I still had to tell you what God told me to tell you no matter how nasty your attitude was. Just because God told you no about your ex-fiancé, it does not mean He is saying no to every man in the universe. He could have another man waiting to be who and what you need him to be in order to get you where God needs you to be."

The waiter interrupted their chat as he approached with their dinner.

"Houston, please forgive me. God is working on me, and I am thankful for that. Yes, I did have a stinky attitude when you met me and even after that on our first few dates. I am truly appreciative He sent you to find me and to talk to me. I am open to whatever He wants to get out and put in me," Eboni said.

"Eboni, just know that you are special, and that God loves you very much. He has someone special for you, too," Houston exclaimed.

"I know you are right. It just takes time," Eboni responded.

"Let me pray over our food so we can eat before it gets cold." He prayed, and they began to eat and continued their conversation.

Meanwhile, Mason and Danielle were sitting on the couch watching a movie with their parents. They were eating popcorn and enjoying some lemonade.

Mason was overly happy as he looked at the ring on Danielle's hand. He thanked God for his soon-to-be wife.

She looked at him and smiled.

They finished the movie and talked for about an hour. As Mason prepared to leave for the evening, he asked Danielle if she needed any paperwork or anything else from the office tomorrow.

She answered, "Yes, bring me the paperwork for Mr. Dennis and Mrs. Fenix. I need to see how I can help them start their investments and what companies they need to invest in."

"I will bring them by tomorrow evening." As always, after he said bye to her parents, he kissed her on her forehead, and he and his parents left out the door.

Downtown, Houston and Eboni finished up their meal. "Eboni, do you want any dessert?"

"Yes. Will you share a slice of cheesecake with me?"

"Sure, I will," he answered.

When the waiter came back to the table to see if they needed dessert, Houston ordered one slice of cheesecake with two forks. A few minutes later, the waiter placed the cheesecake on the table.

Houston stood up and sat in the booth right beside her, and

they ravished the slice of cheesecake.

When they were done, Houston paid for their meals.

"Thank you for a lovely date and for telling me what I needed to hear," Eboni said.

"You are welcome. I just do not want you to stay stuck." He opened the door to her vehicle for her to get in.

"Thank you for everything, Houston. I will call you when I get home."

"You are welcome, and, yes, please call me to let me know you made it home safely," he said. They waved bye as Eboni drove off.

On her journey home, she started to think about all that her and Houston talked about, then she said, "Lord, help me. I don't want to be stuck. I want Mason to be happy, and I want to be happy. God, I have been so evil and mean to Mason and his fiancée. I totally disrespected them and both of their parents. Lord, please forgive me."

By this time, she was in her driveway. In the garage, she sat in her truck and wept while finishing up her prayer. "Lord, please forgive me and show me how and when to ask Mason, his fiancée, and their parents for forgiveness. Oh, God, I acted as if I don't even know You, and they have been nothing but kind to me."

She felt so ashamed. She called Houston to let him know she made it home safely.

He could hear the sadness in her voice. "What's wrong?"

She answered in tears. "Houston, I have been so selfish and evil to Mason and his fiancée. I disrespected them and their parents. How do I even ask them for forgiveness? I have asked God for forgiveness, but how do I ask them?"

"Eboni, you have done the first best thing, and that is admitting that you were wrong, and you asked God to forgive you. He will set up the timing for you to talk to them and ask them for forgiveness. Stop crying and get some rest. I will talk to you tomorrow."

"Thank you, Houston. I will get some rest and talk to you tomorrow. Have a good night," she said.

Inside the house, she got to her bedroom, looked up, and said, "Do I trust You, Lord?" As soon as she got in the bed and her head hit the pillow, she fell asleep.

The next morning there was a shift in how she felt. Eboni woke up feeling so blessed. She felt like the Lord visited her in her sleep and lifted the load she was carrying. She prayed, read her morning's devotion, and got ready for work. She had to be at the salon early, and she was leaving the salon early today.

On her way to the salon, she called Houston to thank him again for listening to her last night and giving her some wisdom in the situation. She also told him how good she felt when she awoke.

He was happy to hear it, and he told her that he would check back with her on his break.

When Eboni got to her salon, her first client was already waiting for her inside.

She walked in, got settled, and attended to her first client.

Later, Mrs. Lane came in to get a shampoo and deep conditioning. When she saw Eboni, she asked, "Okay, young lady, who is he? You are really glowing today."

"Mrs. Lane, it is God. I did what you said and gave everything to Him, and I will not be taking them back."

"Well, I know there is an earthly man in there somewhere too. You can tell me later, but I know he is there."

Eboni smiled as she continued Mrs. Lane's hair. "We will see, Mrs. Lane."

Several miles away, Houston was on his break. Instead of calling Eboni, he sent her a text because he knew she would be busy from what she told him last night at dinner. He asked how was she doing and how her day was going?

When Eboni saw the flash on her phone, she checked, excused herself, and went to the restroom to call him. "HE IS THE ONE," she heard a voice say. She looked around and saw no one in the back hallway. She shook her head and kept walking to the restroom.

"Hi, Eboni, I see you got my text."

"Hi, Houston. Yes, I did get your text. I am doing great, and my day is going even greater," she said.

"You sound so different to me right now, Eboni." You sound peaceful."

"Well, Houston, it is God. I am giving things to Him to handle, and I don't want them back," exclaimed Eboni.

"That's my girl. Just let Him handle it."

She chuckled. "I am letting Him handle it. Anyway, I have to get back to a client, so I will call you when I leave the salon. Talk to you later," she said before hanging up.

Her smile was involuntary and uncontrollable as she walked back up front.

Shannon looked. "Who is he, and don't tell me it is that guy from the mall?"

"What if it is the guy from the mall? Why not him?"

"I thought you wanted Mason," Shannon said.

"Well, some things you have to take and give to God and leave it with Him and go on about your merry way," Eboni responded.

"My sister is maturing and growing up. I like it, E," said Shannon.

Eboni looked at her and smiled even harder.

Eboni was with her last client, and she couldn't stop thinking about all the things she wanted to tell Houston when she called him later.

Houston, too, was in deep thought. He kept looking at the clock in his office, and with only one more hour to go, he was thinking about Eboni and praying that she will allow God to continue the work that He is doing in her. He was also thinking about the things that had happened with him and how he was eager to share them with her.

Back at the salon, Eboni had finished taking care of her last client, and she had cleaned her area. She left out the doors, and as soon as she got in her truck, she called Houston's cell phone. It rang a few times, then went to his voicemail.

About ten minutes after she made it home, her cell phone rang. She looked to see who was calling, and it was Houston returning her call. She answered, "Good evening."

"Good evening, Eboni. Did the rest of your day go well?"

"Yes, it did. God is so good!" she said. "How did the rest of your day go, Houston?"

"It went well. I had to work with a mom and her two children. Both children had to have a tooth pulled, and they were afraid about getting that done. I had to spend about an hour preparing them for the procedure. Yes, that was very interesting," he answered.

"Wow, how interesting!" she said as they continued to tell each other about their day.

"Well, Eboni, I am so happy that the rest of your day was over the top. I pray that Father God continues to do what He wants to do in and through you and that you continue to allow Him to do so."

"Thank you, Houston, and I desire that Father God continues to do what He is doing in me. I don't want Him to stop this process. I feel more refreshed and freer each day," said Eboni.

"Eboni, before we hang up, will you be my guest at my father's place of ministry on Sunday?" asked Houston.

"Sure, I would love to. What is the name of the church and the address?"

He gave her the information, and they said good night to one another. When he got off the phone with her, he heard a voice say, "SHE IS THE ONE!"

He looked up and said, "Thank you, Lord."

Across town, Mason took Danielle the paperwork she asked for. He sat beside her at her breakfast table and asked, "Danielle, is there anything I can help you with on the paperwork? You know we work well as a team."

"I know, and yes, I do need your help. I am having a hard time budgeting their money for several companies they would like to invest in. They have the funds. It's just trying to figure out how much to put in and with what company."

Mason looked at Mr. Dennis's paperwork first. They discussed some strategies for the budget. About thirty minutes later, they finished his paperwork and set his investments in motion.

They did the same thing with Mrs. Fenix's.

"Mason, honey, thank you so much. I just could not get it figured out so they would get the best out of their investments."

"Sweetheart, you are welcome, and I enjoy working with you," Mason explained.

They finished up, and Mason helped her to her recliner in her living room. Before leaving, he made sure she had everything she needed because her parents would be out for a few hours. Once she was good, he left.

When Mason got home, before he could walk through the door of his house, he smelled food. "Mom, what have you done? It smells so good in here. Can I eat now?"

"I just thought you would like a little bit of soul food tonight. I cooked some cabbage with smoked neckbones, yams, macaroni and cheese, fried chicken wings, and hot water cornbread," she said.

"Oh, my goodness, Mom. Thank you." He gave her a big hug.

"Alright, Mason. I'm going to fix you and your father a plate.

I will call you two when your plates are ready.”

“Thanks again, Mom,” he said as he sat in one of his lazy-boy chairs. “Dad, what did you do to her?” Mason asked.

“Son, I just asked for a home-cooked meal, and she said she got me.”

“So, this is what thirty-five years of marriage will do?” Mason asked.

“Yes, Son, with love, respect, and communication.”

“Ron and Mason, the table is set.”

Mason and his dad looked at one another, smiled, and went to the kitchen.

Mrs. Taylor had fixed the plates and cups of sweet, iced tea.

Mr. Taylor prayed, and they began to eat. “Babe, you really did this. Everything is delicious. Thank you.”

She looked at him and smiled. “You are welcome, honey, and thank you for the compliment. I enjoy cooking for two of my favorite fellows.”

They finished eating and talked about their day.

Meanwhile, Danielle had eaten her dinner. Her mother ordered the food before she and her husband went on their date. Following the instructions from Nurse Salters, Danielle took and bathed herself like Nurse Salters showed her and was relaxing in bed.

About one hour later, she heard her parents come in.

Her mother came to her room to check on her. "Danielle, did Mason help you to this room?"

"No, Mom. I wheeled myself back here and took a bath the way Nurse Salters told me to because of the cast. I did not put any pressure on my left leg or foot," Danielle answered.

Mrs. Belkin noticed Danielle not looking like herself. "Sweetheart, what's wrong?"

"Mom, Mason has come over every day this week after work. Today he brought me the paperwork I asked for, and he helped me with it. He told me he would take it back to my office on Monday and scan it into the computer for me. I don't want him missing out on what he would be doing if my leg was not in a cast. I know he loves me without a doubt, but I know that there are other things he would normally be doing," Danielle responded.

"Honey, Mason loves you a lot, and if he wanted to be doing other things, I believe he would be doing them. If he wants to take care of you, then allow him to do that. Do not feel like you are being a burden on anyone. If you were a burden for him it would show.”

“Mom, I know he does, but it’s just hard and my pride is high. Do you know that after this I might not be able to wear my heels, and do you know how tall Mason is?”

Mrs. Belkin looked at Danielle and just smiled. “Honey, listen, you need to shut your pride down and let Mason love you like he wants to love you in the way of visiting you and taking care of you. About the heels, you can always wear short, heeled pumps, and how tall is Mason?”

Danielle responded, “Really, Mom? Mason is six foot five.”

“Honey, you have nothing to worry about.” Mrs. Belkin gave Danielle a hug and a kiss and said to her, “Danielle, baby, don’t let your pride mess things up for you. Good night.”

Danielle looked at her mom. “Yes, ma’am. I won’t let my pride mess things up, Mom. Good night.”

Her mom left out the bedroom door, and Danielle prayed and fell asleep.

CHAPTER 14:
It Is Well With My Soul

It seemed as if there was always something cooking in the Taylors' house. On this specific morning, Mason woke up to a pleasant surprise. He opened his eyes to the aroma of food coming from the kitchen. He immediately thought his mom was up early and cooking up a storm once more.

When he went to the kitchen and opened the door, it was his dad he saw and not his mom. "Dad, it smells good in here. What are you cooking and why?"

"Okay, we have grits, oatmeal, bacon, sausage, pancakes, and waffles. I also have some different juices and a pot of hot coffee. Quintin and Jason are coming over, and you know they enjoy food. See, your mother cooked last night, so I decided to cook this morning."

Mason was waiting for the right time to ask his dad about his burning issue and now seemed perfect. "Dad, do you think I am smothering Danielle by checking on her every day and helping her with different things?" Mason asked.

"Why do you think that, Son?"

"I just feel like I might need to back off a little bit," he answered.

"Why don't you ask Danielle if she feels smothered before you just stop doing what you are already doing?" his dad said.

"I told her I was coming over this afternoon. I will talk to her then. Well, since the guys are coming over, I am going to put some comfortable clothes on. Thank you for helping me out concerning my question about Danielle. I will be back in a moment," Mason said.

Ten blocks over, Mrs. Belkin knocked on Danielle's door. She heard nothing, so she opened the door and walked in. She saw Danielle was still asleep, and she looked so peaceful. She walked around and silently prayed.

Danielle started moving and opened her eyes. "Good morning, Mom. Is everything alright?"

"Everything is alright. Did you rest well last night?"

"Mom, I slept like a baby. Thank you for giving me some wisdom concerning Mason last night. I am truly blessed to have a fiancé like him. Demond was never this interested in caring for me or coming over every day to assist me with anything. Right now, I am truly thankful and grateful for Mason," Danielle exclaimed.

"Sweetheart, that is wonderful. I am so glad that you allowed the Holy Spirit to minister to you. Do you want some breakfast? I have already prepared it."

"Yes, Mom. I want to come to the kitchen, just give me a moment."

"Alright. Your father and I will be waiting for you," Mrs. Belkin said.

Danielle grabbed her house coat from her bedside and placed it on around her shoulders. She shuffled until she was in the wheelchair that was right by her bed.

She wheeled herself to the kitchen and was in awe at all the food her mom had on the table.

"Honey, I will fix your plate, just tell me what you want."

"I would like some grits, sausage, and toast."

"Grits, sausage, and toast coming up, my daughter." She fixed Danielle's plate, prayed, and sat down beside her husband.

"Mom, these grits are so good. Did you do anything different to them?"

"I just added a little bit of American cheese to it and a tablespoon more butter," Mrs. Belkin responded.

"Everything tastes great, dear," Mr. Belkin said.

"Dad and Mom, I am enjoying this breakfast and fellowship, but I need to go get myself together and get dressed for my day. I cannot be in this robe all day. I will have company in a few hours," Danielle exclaimed.

"Yes, darling, go get ready for your fiancé. I will be in there to help you in just a moment," her mom said.

She wheeled herself out of the kitchen to her bedroom.

"I see she is letting her pride go," said Mr. Belkin, with a smirk on his face.

"I am praying that is what's happening. Last night she was not being the confident Danielle that I know she is. I'll be right back, babe. I'm going to help her get dressed," Mrs. Belkin exclaimed.

At Mason's house, Quintin and Jason had arrived. They greeted Mason.

"I see you guys are hungry. Huh?" They all laughed, and Mason said, "Let's go eat."

"Mrs. Taylor, you have done it again. You always do a good, big breakfast," Quintin said.

"Thank you, Quintin, but Mr. Taylor did breakfast this morning."

"Wow, Mr. Taylor, you can burn," said Quintin.

"Quintin, son, thank you," said Mr. Taylor.

They all chuckled.

"Okay, I believe I have eaten enough for breakfast, lunch, and maybe dinner. I am stuffed," Mason said jokingly.

They all agreed the food was filling and tasty.

"Fellas, are you two ready to go for a thirty-minute walk before we go to the gym to get our work out on?" Mason asked.

"Yes, because this breakfast makes me want to go lay down somewhere," said Jason.

"Dad, Mom, thank you. We must leave for a little while."

Mrs. Taylor looked at her husband and asked him if he was going with them this morning.

"No. I took a walk earlier this morning, and I want some alone time with you." They shared a kiss. "I will get this dishwasher started and meet you in the living room."

In the living room, she looked to see what movies Mason had in his collection. There was one that she couldn't remember if she had seen or not. The movie was *Courageous*. She wanted to see it because it was by the Kendrick brothers, and every movie she had seen by them she had enjoyed.

Mr. Taylor came out of the kitchen and stood behind her. He placed his arms around her waist and told her he was so thankful for her and that she knew how to keep him smiling.

"Ron, don't get things started now, and have you seen this movie before?" Mrs. Taylor asked.

He looked at the movie "I don't think I have. Do you want to watch it?"

She answered, "Yes, please."

She started the movie, and they got cozy in each other's arms.

Ten blocks away from Mason's house, Danielle's parents were getting ready to run some errands. "Danielle, we are getting ready to go to a few stores. Would you like to go, or do you want to stay home?"

"If you and Dad will help me in and out of the truck, sure, I would love to go," answered Danielle. She quickly got dressed in a beautiful yellow sundress with her sandals and did her makeup.

"Let's go," Mr. Belkin said. He wheeled Danielle to his Tahoe and helped her get in. All three rolled out to the market where they picked up some salmon, steak, chicken, and vegetables. They also got a little snack to eat while they were walking around shopping. Next, they went to the supermarket to buy rice, flour, sweeteners, and fruits.

By this time, Danielle's arm was getting tired and sore from wheeling herself around in the stores.

"Alright, sweetheart, I believe we need to get our baby home so she can get a little rest before Mason comes over," said Mr. Belkin.

They paid for their items, loaded them into the back of the SUV, and headed home.

"Dad and Mom, for some reason I am excited about Mason coming over today. I am more excited today than I have been all week."

"That's great, dear. Ask the Lord to help you keep that excitement even when things are not going the way you think they should go," Mrs. Belkin exclaimed.

Then they heard what was playing on the radio, the song "It is Well with My Soul."

Danielle proclaimed, "Yes, it is well with my soul." She looked out the window at the scenery, reminiscing the rest of the way home.

Across town, the boys were at the gym.

"Quintin and Jason, I am finally crushing this weight bench. I am up to two hundred fifty pounds now," explained Mason.

"That's what I am talking about, bro. Yeah," Quintin and Jason responded.

"Mason, I meant to ask you earlier, how is Danielle?" asked Jason.

"She is doing well. I just feel like I have been smothering her by going by to visit her every day this week."

"Mason, umm, what makes you think that you are smothering her? Did she tell you that you are smothering her?" Quintin asked.

"No, she did not tell me I was smothering her. Yesterday when I took her some paperwork she needed to work on, I asked her if she needed some help with it because we work well together on different things at the office. She seemed a little hesitant about me helping her. Danielle is an amazing woman, and I don't want her to think that I pity her or feel sorry for her because she is on crutches or in a wheelchair for the moment. She is still amazing to me, and she is most beautiful right now. I can't wait to spend the rest of my life with her."

"Okay Mason, I feel you. You know Pam and Marla enjoy talking with Danielle. They say they are excited about the wedding, and they are waiting patiently for that day," Jason said.

"That is so sweet of them. Danielle says she enjoys talking to and being out with them. She says they are a major encouragement to her. With that being said, are we done? Because I need to go and see Danielle. I told her I would be over to check on her sometime this afternoon," said Mason.

"Yeah, man. Let's go. You have to take care of your girl," said Jason.

They grabbed their towels and water bottles and went back to Mason's house. Once they got to Mason's house, Quintin and Jason went home.

CHAPTER 15:

I Love You With The Love Of The Lord

When Mason arrived at Danielle's home, she was asleep. She opened her eyes just to see Mason sitting in a chair on the side of her bed. "Hi, sweetie. I asked your parents if I could come and pretty much watch you rest. I hope that was okay?"

"Mason, I am glad to see you," Danielle said as she sat up in the bed.

"Danielle, do you feel that I am smothering you by coming to visit and check on you every day?"

"No Mason. I was thinking that I was taking you away from other things you might want to do when you come by to check on me."

"Wow. Sweetheart, we were both thinking differently. Danielle, you are my amazing woman, and I am waiting patiently to spend the rest of my life with you. I love you with the love of the Lord, Danielle."

Teary-eyed, she said, "Mason, I just did not want to be the reason why you were not doing the things you would be doing if I did not have the cast on my leg and arm. Like on Mondays you go out with the boys and on Tuesday you go to the gym and so on. I just don't want you to put things on hold because of me."

"Darling, you know what? This morning, I had breakfast with my parents and Quintin and Jason. Afterwards, the boys and I went for a thirty-minute walk through the neighborhood, and then we went to the gym. So, I still do other things. I still have to make sure that you are good, and I am thankful that we can and do communicate with one another when something is bothering us."

"Thanks, Mason. I am working on this pride thing," she said.

"Danielle, would you like to go to the park down the street for a little bit?"

"Sure, will you help me into my chair?"

"Sure, I will," Mason said. He helped her into the wheelchair.

As he wheeled her into the living room where her parents were, she told them the plans to go to the park. "Dad and Mom, Mason and I are going to the park for a little bit."

"Okay. Have a good time and enjoy the time with each other."

Mason and Danielle went two blocks down the sidewalk to the park. While Mason was pushing her to the park, he told her how Quintin and Jason asked about her and how Pam and Marla are waiting patiently on the wedding and to see her again for a girls' night out.

Danielle also shared with him about her going to the market and to the supermarket with her parents earlier. She also shared how she planned to keep up her healthy eating habits and how she felt a little depressed earlier in the week because of the cast being on her leg.

At the park, Mason pushed Danielle around different areas so she could enjoy the view. They sat around for an hour or so watching the birds and people until it was time for them to go home.

On the way home, Danielle was excited to tell Mason she would be present in church tomorrow. Mason was overjoyed.

After making it back home, Mrs. Belkin offered them a snack. She made them a delicious bowl of fruit. Mason and Danielle really loved fruits, so they were surprised and happy to see the two bowls when her mother came out of the kitchen.

"Thanks, Mama Belkin. I love fruit," said Mason.

"You both are welcome. Enjoy."

When they were finished, Mason took both bowls to the kitchen and went back to the living room to chill.

After a few minutes, Mason looked at Danielle and told her he had to go, and he would see her at service tomorrow along with her parents.

"Yes, we will be there," Danielle said.

He kissed her on the forehead, gave her dad and mom a hug, and walked out the door to his vehicle.

Her dad walked out with him, and they spoke for a few minutes before Mason drove off.

For dinner that same day, Mrs. Belkin baked the salmon they bought at the Fresh Market. She cooked some basmati rice and steamed asparagus.

When dinner was ready, they ate and chatted.

"Mom, this salmon is so delicious. What seasonings did you use?" Danielle asked.

"Honey, I looked at your spice rack and just started using the different seasonings you had."

"Well, Mom, it is good."

"Thanks, sweetheart," said her mother.

They finished dinner, washed up the dishes, and prepared for bed.

After everything was finished Danielle said, "Goodnight, Mom, and Dad. I am going to get ready and go to bed. Mom, will you come help me get dressed for bed, please?"

"Yes, baby, I will, and I am going to get ready for bed too. I feel a little exhausted."

Danielle and her mom left the kitchen while Mr. Belkin was still in the living room watching television.

Later, Mrs. Belkin went back to the living room and sat beside him on the couch. They shared a kiss and looked into each other's eyes. "Ralph, I love you."

"Baby, I love you more." Mr. Belkin turned off the television and the living room light, and they went to bed.

At Mason's home, he pulled up and saw his parents sitting out on the swing on his porch. "Okay, what are you two up to?"

They looked at one another, shared a kiss, looked back at him, and said, "Nothing."

"Okay, I see you two need alone time. I will be in the kitchen fixing us something for dinner." Mason walked into the house and changed into a pair of sweats and a faith t-shirt. He washed his hands and looked in the refrigerator to see what he could cook for dinner. He saw that his mom had taken out some chicken wings. He also found, in the cabinet, two cans of cream of chicken soup. He decided to fix baked chicken wings.

Halfway through the baking process, he emptied the two cans of cream of chicken soup over them. Added to that, he cooked some jasmine rice and some fresh green beans and a pitcher of sweet tea.

His parents were still outside watching God's creation. When the food was ready, he went to go get them, but they both were asleep. His dad's head was laid back on the top of the back of the swing, and his mom was in his dad's arm with her head resting on his chest. He stood there watching them and prayed that he and Danielle could have this type of friendship/relationship. He said to himself, "They have been married for almost forty years and still love each other like they just met."

He also thought about a conversation he recently had with his dad concerning his and his mom's relationship. His dad told him that every day with his mom was sweeter than the day before. "That is the type of relationship I want with Danielle." He said it so loudly it startled his dad.

"Mason, what's wrong, Son?"

"Oh, nothing. Just watching you and Mom sleep on the swing. Dinner is ready whenever you two want to eat."

"Okay! Sylvia, honey, wake up. Mason said the food is ready."

She woke up and stretched. "Oh, my goodness! Ron, what time is it and how long have we been out here?"

"Baby, it is only fifteen minutes after six. We have only been out here a couple of hours," Mr. Taylor answered.

"Let's go in and eat so we can go to bed," said Mrs. Taylor. They went inside the house, and Mr. Taylor locked the door behind them as they walked into the kitchen.

"Mason, it smells good in here. What did you cook?"

"I smothered some chicken wings in some cream of chicken soup. I also cooked some jasmine rice and green beans with sweet tea."

"Thank you, Son. I just want to eat, shower, and go to bed," Mrs. Taylor said.

They ate and conversed until it was time for bed.

In the bedroom, Mr. Taylor had already taken a shower and

was in bed reading some things he believed God wanted him to minister on in a week or two. Mrs. Taylor was out of the shower and dressed for bed.

Mr. Belkin had agreed to preach again tomorrow, so Mr. Taylor was in preparation mode. Thirty minutes later, he finished reading what he wrote and looked over to find his wife fast asleep. He slid down into the bed in order not to wake her, and then he, too, headed to sleep.

CHAPTER 16:
God, I See You Moving

There was something unusual about this Sunday as everyone got ready for morning services. Mason got up and prayed like he normally would, but this morning he felt something different as he interceded. It was as if he was beyond full and was about to explode with the joy of the Lord. He began to worship and sing songs of praise to the True and Living God he served.

His dad walked by the room, and he too knew something uncommon was happening. He looked up and said, "God, I know You are going to move today. Be glorified in Your moving. Have Your way today, Lord."

Sunday School started at nine o'clock, and so they headed out for church. Sunday school was such as blessing, and Mason and his family expected God to take them higher during morning worship.

Shortly before praise and worship started, Mason went to the foyer so he could assist the greeters in welcoming the congregation as they came into the sanctuary. As he was serving, he saw from afar Danielle's dad pushing her towards the building and her mother walking alongside them. He held his composure and kept greeting those who were coming.

"Good morning, Dad, and Mom Belkin. Good morning, Danielle," he said as he hugged them. "Do you need me to help you with anything?"

"Sure, Son. If you will, ensure Danielle and my wife are seated up front for me." said Mr. Belkin as he left to go prepare for service.

Mason did as he was asked and took Danielle and Mrs. Belkin to their seats.

The praise and worship started promptly at ten o'clock, and there was such a glory that fell as the songs went up.

Mason sat with Danielle by a side door just in case she needed to go to the restroom. That location was also perfect because she could elevate the leg that was in the cast.

Danielle sat and worshipped. Clapping her hands and rocking in the wheelchair the whole time.

Once worship was over, Mr. Taylor got up and welcomed the visitors and blessed the Lord for the praise and worship time. The announcements were made, followed by a song of mediation before the "Bread of Life." Mr. Taylor had the privilege of presenting the guest speaker, Mr. Belkin.

Mason and Danielle looked at each other and smiled.

Mr. Belkin preached a powerful sermon on love and forgiveness.

This was the word Mason needed, and now he understood why he was feeling like he was about to explode with joy this morning. He knew that he had to love and forgive Eboni. He repented, "Lord, I forgive her, and I pray she forgives me."

"Mason, what's wrong?" asked Danielle.

"I will tell you later, honey." Then he thought about what he needed to talk to Danielle about. He prayed she would be open to a date change.

At the end of service, Mason sat with Danielle while their parents spoke to everyone before they left. Some of the members of the congregation even came over to speak with Mason and Danielle.

Church was now empty, so Mason helped Danielle into her dad's truck. "Hey Danielle, you know my mom cooked a meal for all of us. We will head to my house to gather everything, and we will be over shortly," he said.

"That is so kind of her. Mason, on a different note, I am so excited that our special day is coming up soon," Danielle said as Mason helped her into the vehicle.

Mason and his parents went back to his house to change and pack up the food Mrs. Taylor had cooked. "Dad, Mom, are you ready? I am taking the food out to the truck."

His dad yelled, "We will be out in a few minutes."

Ten minutes away, Houston was talking to Eboni, wondering where she was. "You were supposed to be here five minutes ago. I will see you when you get here."

"Okay, Houston, I'll be there shortly." A few minutes later she drove up to the church where Houston was patiently waiting on her so they could walk in together.

Mr. Livingston, Houston's father, pastored a church that was only minutes from where Mr. Taylor pastored. They walked in while praise and worship were going on.

After the praise and worship time, Pastor Livingston got up to welcome a few special guests, followed by announcements. Just like Mr. Belkin, Pastor Livingston ministered to the congregation about forgiveness. All that Eboni needed to hear, he ministered.

Every now and then she would poke Houston's arm and whisper to him, "Did you tell him about our conversations?"

He whispered, "No, I did not."

She just looked at him and chuckled.

He smiled back at her as they continued to listen to the message.

During the altar call, Eboni asked Houston if he would go to the altar with her. They walked up together. Eboni wanted to get things right. She desired forgiveness.

While at the altar, she asked the Lord to show her how to ask those she hurt to forgive her and the right timing. At the altar, she wept as Mr. Livingston prayed for her and Houston.

After the service, Houston took Eboni over to meet his parents. They stood in line to wait for their turn to greet them.

"Houston, do you think this is the right time?" Eboni asked.

"Yes. Why not now? We are friends until God brings us closer, right?"

"Yes, you are right."

As they got closer, Mr. Livingston looked up and saw her with him and had a certain look on his face with a smile.

"Mom and Dad, this is Eboni Cutler."

"God bless you, Eboni. I am Pastor Houston Livingston III,

and this is my wife, Lisa Livingston. It is a pleasure to meet you."

"It is a pleasure to meet you too, sir and ma'am," Eboni said.

"Would you two like to go out to lunch with us?" Mrs. Livingston asked.

Houston looked at Eboni and asked her if she was available for lunch.

"Sure. I can tag along," she said.

"Okay, Eboni you can ride with me in my truck, and I will bring you back to get your truck later."

At the restaurant, Houston and Eboni talked to his mom and dad.

"So, young lady, tell us how you met our son, or how did our son talk you into this?" Mr. Livingston laughed.

"Well, he was very straight forward, and he did not have one of those tired lines. Thank you, Jesus, for that because tired lines are a turn off for me. After making it past that first step, he invited me out to dinner, and I agreed."

"That's my boy! You make your parents proud," said Mr. Livingston with a laugh in his voice.

"Thanks, dad. I learned from the best."

At this time, the waiter brought their food to the table. They got acquainted as they ate, and Mr. Livingston cleared up the bill once they were done.

Outside the restaurant, they talked some more. "Thank you so much for the invitation to have lunch with you. I really enjoyed myself, and it was a pleasure meeting you both," said Eboni.

"It was a pleasure meeting and talking with you, too, sweetheart," said Mr. Livingston.

"Thanks Dad and Mom for the invite. I will see you at the house later."

"You are welcome, Son. See you later."

Houston walked Eboni to his truck. He opened the door for her.

Eboni looked at him in amazement. As she gazed into Houston's eyes, she heard a voice saying, "This is your husband." She was stunned! "Did you hear that?"

"Hear what?" he asked.

"Never mind. I might be just hearing things." She got in the truck, and he closed the door. "I really enjoyed lunch. It was a pleasure meeting your parents," Eboni said.

"I am glad you enjoyed it. So, have you thought about or has God shown you what to do concerning being unstuck?" asked Houston as he drove.

"I have been praying about it, and I know I have to first ask Mason and his family for forgiveness. The question is when! I just need God to tell me when."

By this time, they were back at the church by her truck.

"Thank you again for accepting my invitation to visit my father's church and for the last-minute request to join us for lunch," Houston said.

"You are so welcome."

He got out and went around to open her door.

As she stepped out, she heard the voice again, telling her that he was her husband. She smiled as he closed the door and walked her to her truck.

"I will call you later on this evening, Eboni."

"Okay, I will talk to you then," she replied.

He got in his car, and they went their separate ways.

Back at Danielle's house, lunch was served. "Mom, you really outdid yourself again today. This meatloaf is glorious," said Mason.

"Yes, it is, Sylvia. You must give me your recipe. Mine is good, but this is perfect and different," Mrs. Belkin shared.

"Normally, I don't give out my recipes, but for you I will make an exception," Mrs. Taylor explained.

Danielle took the floor and decided to pour her heart out. "I want to thank everyone for all the help you have given me over the past week. To my parents, for dropping things they had to do to bring me my work from the office. Thanks for fixing my meals and helping out around the house. Thank you, Mr. and Mrs. Taylor, for loving me as if I am already married to your son. Last but never least, thank you to my fiancé, Mason, who keeps going above and beyond to help me. Not just here at home but also at work," she said while looking at him and gently holding his hand.

They looked at her, smiled and said, "You are welcome."

They continued talking to one another and enjoying their lunch.

"So, Danielle, can we go and talk?" Mason asked. He wheeled

her into the living room. "Danielle, you know next to loving God, I love you. I know without a doubt you are my wife to be. I also know that you desire to walk down the aisle on your own and not with assistance from a wheelchair, crutches, or a cane. What do you think about us changing our wedding date?" he asked.

Danielle was moved to tears. "Mason, you are so thoughtful. I would love the date to be changed. I have been thinking and praying about this since the accident. I just did not know how to talk to you about it."

"Danielle, this is how I know our union is of God. I did not know how you would respond either. I was struggling to say what I needed to say to you."

"Well, what date are you looking at?" she asked.

"I was thinking about January twelfth."

"I will have to check because I believe that is the same day my cousin Renee is getting married. I will check. What about the first weekend in February?" she asked.

"Danielle, I want to be your husband, not your forever fiancé."

"Really, Mason, it is only two more months. We have waited this long. We can wait another two months," she said.

He lamented, "Danielle, I just did not want to wait that long to marry you, and yes, I know that patience is a virtue. I am going to have to work on this."

"Mason, look at it like this: God is giving us time to get some more things together, and I see we both need to practice patience," she said as they laughed.

"Now we have to let our family and friends know that our wedding date will be announced later because we decided to change it due to an unfortunate event," he said while looking at her cast.

Across town, Eboni was praying. "Lord, show me when to talk to Mason, his fiancée, and their parents. I have to get this right if Houston is my husband. Lord, have You told him? Lord, I need more of You." She continued in prayer as she drove to her brother's house.

Houston, however, was on his way to his dad and mom's house. He called his dad on the way to see if everything was ok and how he felt about the day.

"Everything is fine, Son. I really enjoyed meeting and talking to Miss Eboni today. I need you to really pray and ask God what He is saying about this young lady."

"Dad, I have been praying, and I truly believe she is my wife.

To be honest, I know she is my wife. I am waiting for God's timing before I move towards a relationship, though."

"Wow, Son. When I saw her today, I said to myself, 'She is the one for him.' Even your mother said, 'Honey, you know that Eboni is that boy's wife. We have another daughter," Mr. Livingston shared.

"Dad, I love it when you and Mom confirm things for me. It lets me know that I am on the right track with my Father, God."

"Son, you have matured so much in the last two years. Not only from the standpoint of being a man but you have also matured in God."

Both men decided to finish up the conversation when Houston got to the house.

"Alright, Son, I will see you in a few."

Houston hung up and started to pray. "Lord, thank You for confirmation through my parents. Now, God, You set up the time and place for this relationship to move further."

By this time, he was pulling into his parents' driveway. When he got to the house, he saw his mom out on the porch, swinging back and forth.

He parked and walked up. "I see someone is really enjoying this day," Houston said to his mom.

"Yes, I am," she said, smiling and rocking. "Come here, Son, and let's have a talk."

He went over and sat beside her.

Meanwhile, Eboni had made it to her brother Alex's home.

"Hey, Sis, come on in. We just got in from church. Are you hungry? And where are you coming from all dressed up and looking cute?"

"I'm coming from church, boy. Can I talk to you and Kathleen in private, please?"

"Sure, let us get the children settled in here at the table first," Alex said. They got the children settled at the table in the kitchen, and then they went to the living room where Eboni was sitting. "So, what's going on, Sis?"

She answered, "Remember the guy I went out to eat with a few months ago? Well, I believe he is my husband-to-be."

Alex slid forward into the love seat. "What? Eboni, we have been through this before. What is your problem?"

"Alex, it is not the same thing. I went to lunch with him and his parents today, and twice I heard the Lord say that he is my husband, audibly," Eboni said.

Alex shook his head. "That's what you said about Mason. Will this be the same?"

"No, this is different. I should not have tried to hold on to Mason like I did. I asked the Lord to help my heart and change me concerning that situation, and that is what He did, and I am very thankful for that," Eboni responded. "

So, you are not mad at Mason anymore and I do not have to hear about how he is your husband anymore, right?"

"Yes, Alex you are right, but you do have to hear about Houston Livingston IV."

"Is this the new guy? Can you tell us a little about him?" Alex said.

"Firstly, he is a man of God, and he gives great advice. He is six feet three inches tall and weighs one hundred seventy-five pounds. He is a dentist and some celebrities come to him for dental work. He lives in a very nice neighborhood. He has a four-bedroom, three-bathroom home. I have not seen it yet, but I plan to have dinner with him at his home one day this week," Ebony responded.

"Alex, I believe she is serious. Look at her face when she speaks about him. Her eyes glisten," said Kathleen.

"Yes, I see that. Alright, Sis, if this is your husband then what about Mason?"

She answered, "Alex and Kathleen, I was holding on to Mason for too long. I was trying to force him to be back in a relationship with me, and this was not of God. I wanted something that the Lord did not want to happen. Two weeks ago, while I was talking with Houston, the Lord revealed to me how rude and selfish I had been to Mason, his fiancée, and their parents."

"What do you mean, their parents?" Alex asked.

"Brother, it is so embarrassing that I don't want to talk about the things I did."

"Alright, Sis, what do you need us to do?"

"I just need you and Kathleen to support me while I am pressing to do what I know God told me to do."

"Eboni, you know you always have our support. I see that the Lord is doing something in your heart. I can see that you are allowing Him to make the changes in you," said Kathleen.

"Thank you, guys. I greatly appreciate the both of you. If

Mom and Dad were alive, I would be talking to them, and I know they would be proud."

"Sis, just continue to let God do what He is doing in you. The Bible says, 'He who has begun a good work in you is faithful to complete it,'" Alex said.

"Well, that is all I needed." She stood, and they hugged. "Alright, you can go eat now. Give my nieces and nephew some love for me."

"We will, Sis. You take care. If I don't call you later, I will call you tomorrow," Alex said. He walked her to the door while Kathleen went to the kitchen to check on the children and to fix her and Alex's plate.

Meanwhile, back at Danielle's house, everyone was super full.

"I am so stuffed. I don't know if I need a meal like this again anytime soon. I am so glad you all thought of bringing us food to eat," said Mr. Belkin.

"We are honored, and it is our pleasure to serve you all today. Especially after how good you fed us earlier today with that word," said Mr. Taylor.

Mason's phone rang and interrupted the chatter. He looked at the number and hesitated to answer it. "Good evening," he answered.

The voice on the other end of the line said, "Mason, please don't hang up."

"Why shouldn't I, Eboni?"

"Mason, please forgive me for holding on to you and for trying to force you to love me when I knew that was not what God wanted. I have been very disrespectful to you, your fiancée, and both of your parents. Will you forgive me?"

"Yes, Eboni. I forgive you."

"Thank you. When will you see your parents again?" she asked.

"I am with them now. We are having a late lunch with Danielle and her parents," he answered.

"Well, will you please put your phone on speaker so I can speak to everyone?"

"Hold on! Alright, you're on speaker now."

"Good afternoon, everyone. I just want to ask all of you to forgive me for acting as if I didn't know God. I apologize for being selfish when it came to Mason and Danielle's happiness. Please forgive me for all the problems I have caused. Mason and Danielle, I pray your wedding and marriage will be blessed.”

“We forgive you, Eboni,” they all said.

Mason took the phone off speaker, placed it to his ear, and said, “Thank you, Eboni. You be blessed also today.”

They hung up.

Mason looked up and said, “God, I see you moving.”

Mrs. Taylor said, “Wow, look at how God works. I had been praying for her and that the Lord makes the necessary changes.”

Across town, Eboni called Houston.

“Hi, what’s going on, Eboni?”

“I did it with God’s help,” Eboni said.

“Did what, Eboni?”

“I asked Mason, Danielle, and their parents to forgive me,” she said.

“That is great. I am so happy for you. Now, you can move on and be free.”

"Yes, I can, and right now I feel so liberated," she said.

This was a day of freedom and victory for Eboni, Mason, and Danielle.

Mason and Danielle agreed to be married in February at his dad's place of worship.

At a restaurant across town, Houston proposed to Eboni, and of course, she said yes!

Houston and Eboni began their journey to marriage. They both agreed to counseling and   taking things slowly at a pace.

Mason, Danielle, Eboni, and Houston began to understand that waiting on God for the things they desire to have was best. Isaiah chapter forty and verse thirty-one reads *"But they that wait upon the LORD shall renew their strength, they shall mount up with wings as eagles; they shall run, and not be weary; and they shall walk, and not faint."* Mason did not faint during the time Eboni caused the disturbance at Danielle's home. Mason received the mate God had for him and the mate God had for Eboni found her. So, waiting was both of their blessings. Waiting can be a hard task, but when you wait, oh the blessings you will receive.

In book one Mason finds the mate God had set aside for him and the mate God had set aside for Eboni finds her. In book two we are invited to two amazing weddings. Mason and Danielle enjoy a wonderful honeymoon, but things intensify when Danielle becomes pregnant. Houston and Eboni enjoy a great and amazing honeymoon, but when the honeymoon is over and reality hits home, can Eboni handle the reality she has to face? See what happens next in book two.

Conclusion

In conclusion, I pray that everyone who reads a copy of this book will experience transformation as they make God the center of all their relationships. Also, I hope there will be clarity as to how prayer is a vital component of all relationships.

As I wrote this book, I remember my firsthand experience with praying fervently for A Love of a Lifetime partner. When I was in Junior High school, we had a sex education class. Around the same time, I can remember many young girls my age was becoming pregnant. I was scared straight. This caused me to avoid talking to or touching boys at all costs. On one occasion, I recall having a conversation with my cousin during our lunch period. He insisted that I needed to give in to having sex and exploring intimacy. He alluded to the fact that "no one wanted any old stuff." I assured him that God had someone unique for me and they would be happy with me after we were married.

This was how I developed a passion for prayer. I began to pray and ask the Lord to help me maintain my innocence and to also find a partner I desired. I was happy to be a virgin and my prayer was for a husband who also shared my sentiments. God gave me just that. Around mid-March of 1995, I found out a certain young man was interested in me. The first thing that happened was, his parents came to meet my parents. They wanted to let my parents know their son was interested in marrying me. Apparently that meeting went well because the next weekend they brought their son to meet my parents. On that day he proposed to me, and I said yes! He was exactly what I prayed for. We were married in December of 1995.

My story might be different from yours but be cognizant of the fact that God has that special someone for you. It is His will and desire for you to experience unconditional love. Just keep God first and He will do the rest. Be blessed.

www.ingramcontent.com/pod-product-compliance
Lightning Source LLC
Chambersburg PA
CBHW051522150726
47997CB00001B/347